LEGAL INFORMATION: WHAT IT IS AND WHERE TO FIND IT

Peter Clinch

The Aslib Know How Series

Editor : Sylvia P Webb

THE ASSOCIATION FOR INFORMATION MANAGEMENT

Published in 1995 by
Aslib, The Association for Information Management
Information House
20-24 Old Street
London
EC1V 9AP

***

British Library Cataloguing in Publication Data
A catalogue record for this book is available from the British Library
ISBN 0 85142 335 3

Series Editor - Sylvia P. Webb

Sylvia Webb is a well known consultant, author and lecturer in the information management field. Her first book 'Creating an Information Service' was published by Aslib and has sold in over forty countries. She has experience of working in both the public and private sectors, ranging from public libraries to national and international organisations. She has also been a lecturer at Ashridge Management College, specialising in management and inter-personal skills, which led to her second book, 'Personal Development in Information Work', also published by Aslib. She has served on a number of government advisory bodies and is Chair of the Information and Library Services Lead Body which develops National Vocational Qualifications (NVQs) for the LIS profession. She is actively involved in professional education with Aslib and the Library Association and is also a former Vice-President of the Institute of Information Scientists. As well as being editor of this series, Sylvia Webb has also written two of the Know How Guides: 'Making a charge for library and information services' and 'Preparing a guide to your library and information service'.

A list of titles in the Aslib Know How Series appears on the back cover of this volume.

Contents

1. Introduction

The purpose of this book is to provide an introductory guide to legal information and how to find it. It is designed for library and information services (LIS) staff who do not have a law background, but who wish to undertake basic law reference and enquiry work with confidence.

The law pervades every area of human activity: business, commerce, industry, central government and local authority operations, science, technology, and even the arts and humanities (for example, the law relating to entertainment, literary publication, defamation (libel and slander), the operation of museums, art galleries and libraries). It is highly likely that at some stage in the career of a LIS professional, he or she will need to trace or acquire information on the law.

This book is not meant to take a comprehensive view of the subject. Wherever possible details of further sources are provided. Law librarianship and legal information are vast topics, but it is hoped that this 'sketch' of the subject will go some way to dispelling the mystery and sense of apprehension LIS staff may feel when dealing with legal information.

The rest of the book is in four parts:

- chapter 2 is concerned with how to find a law collection and also explains some basic characteristics of legal information and research;
- chapter 3 describes the major legal information sources for the British Isles. Chapter 4 describes key sources covering the European Community, Continental Europe, Australia, Canada, the United States and International Law;
- chapter 5 provides contact information on the major law database providers, publishers and bookshops mentioned in this book, and details of the major law special interest associations and groups in the UK and abroad for LIS personnel.

I acknowledge the support of the Library Service of the University of Wales College of Cardiff in the compilation of this guide. I am also indebted to my present and past work colleagues and customers for their insights into law library and information work - there is always something new to learn!

2. Finding and using a law collection

2.1 Finding a law collection

The best guide to finding a law collection in the British Isles is the *Directory of British and Irish Law Libraries,* compiled for the British and Irish Association of Law Librarians (BIALL) by Judith Barden (Hebden Bridge: Legal Information Resources Ltd., 4th ed., 1992. At the time of writing, a new edition is being prepared.) The Association is *the* special interest group for law librarians - see chapter 5 for details of how to join. The directory lists over 400 law libraries with brief details of the size of their collection, opening hours, etc., but most importantly, a named contact. All the entries are arranged geographically, so it is quite easy to trace if there is a law library nearby. The directory includes libraries in universities, the law courts, government, law firms, the public library service and special libraries. Not all are open to non-members, and some may have very specialised collections, so it is worth enquiring before setting off to use them.

There are about 80 universities that teach law in the British Isles. These universities are likely to have the largest law collections in the geographical area. The collections are designed to serve the needs of the university's students and staff and may not contain some types of material required in the practice as opposed to the study of law. Big does not necessarily mean comprehensive. University libraries are open to the general public to consult but not to borrow. Some university libraries operate external membership schemes for individuals and/or professional, business and commercial organisations. The terms and costs of individual schemes vary, but they usually permit members to borrow from the library and, in some instances, obtain help from library staff in tracing and obtaining information. Often a particular member of the library staff has responsibility for the law collection. Because of this specialisation, university law librarians will probably be the best able to advise on how to solve more complicated legal information needs. Ask your local university law librarian if the university provides a corporate external membership scheme.

The public libraries of the British Isles should not be overlooked. The large central libraries of most cities will have modest law collections. They will probably be strongest in the collection of Government publications, such as Acts of Parliament (or, in Ireland, Acts of the Oireachtas) and Statutory Instruments. Through their local history/local studies collections, they may have copies of local Acts of Parliament and books on ancient local laws and customs (e.g. tin, lead and coal mining, waterways) which can still be relevant in modern disputes over rights to land and property. Public libraries are usually weakest in the collection of the reports of cases heard before the courts.

Outside the British Isles, professional associations for law librarians similar to BIALL may have prepared directories of libraries, for example: the *Directory of the Canadian Association of Law Libraries* (Toronto). It could be useful to contact an association itself for help in tracing an appropriate library: for example the American Association of Law Librarians (Chicago), or the Australian Law Librarians' Group (Perth).

2.2 What to know before you start law research

There are five valuable points to bear in mind before you start to use a law collection:

- parliaments or legislatures - the bodies responsible for making or amending laws - have their own 'sphere of influence' or, more correctly, 'jurisdiction', limited to a particular geographical area. For example, the law of the United Kingdom of Great Britain and Northern Ireland comprises three distinct jurisdictions: England & Wales, Scotland, and Northern Ireland. Note that the Channel Islands and the Isle of Man are *not* included in these jurisdictions. The concept of jurisdiction has implications for the way in which the search for legal information is conducted.
- whilst the United Kingdom comprises several different jurisdictions, there are many similarities between the way these three legal systems are structured and operate. Consequently there are similarities in the information they produce. But the legal systems and information sources of countries such as England, France, Poland and Japan, for example, are quite different to each other. You need to be aware that there are several families of legal systems, so that knowledge of the similarities between the members of each family will assist your information searching, as much as knowledge of the distinctions between each family.
- there is one constant in the law - change: new laws are enacted, courts interpret them and settle legal disputes, new codes and standards of practice are authorised. You will need to be aware of this and ensure that when you provide legal information it is up to date.
- not all legal documents are published. For example, the courts hear and decide on tens of thousands of cases each year, but only a small percentage of those decisions is published. Very occasionally you may be asked to trace unpublished information. You will need to know the most effective ways of obtaining it.
- lawyers often use abbreviations and special forms of citation to refer to a particular legal source or type of document - indexes to these are available and will enable you to correctly identify the information required.

Let us explore these five points in turn.

2.3 Jurisdiction

As was noted above, each legislature creates legislation applying to a particular geographical area or jurisdiction. Each jurisdiction has its own court structures, hierarchies, procedures and traditions. The courts administer justice and interpret the law made by the legislature. The United Kingdom comprises three distinct jurisdictions. Some Acts or parts of Acts of Parliament apply only to England and Wales, some to England, Wales and Scotland, and yet others to England, Wales, Scotland and Northern Ireland. For example, parts of the Local Government Finance Act 1992, which abolished community charges and replaced them with the council tax, apply to England and Wales only, parts to Scotland only, and none of the Act to Northern Ireland. Chapter 3 of this book explains where in British publications information about jurisdiction will be found.

Overlaying what might be termed the domestic UK jurisdiction are the Treaties, Regulations, Directives and other legislation of the European Community (EC), supplemented by the decisions of the European Court of Justice. The EC aims to harmonise laws between member states. The main instruments are EC Regulations and Directives. So, LIS staff need to be aware of the European Community dimension to UK law and be able to search EC materials effectively. For definitions of terms such as 'European Union' see page 33.

Jurisdiction is also significant when finding legal information about countries with state and federal legal systems, as in the United States. You can waste unacceptable amounts of time in paper and electronic sources if you are uncertain whether you are searching for state or federal law, or law involving more than one state.

Implications for LIS staff:

- when dealing with a subject enquiry make sure you know for which jurisdiction the information is required

- make sure that the publication or database you are using covers that jurisdiction

- a law library usually contains most material on the jurisdiction in which it is located, and much less about other jurisdictions. Don't be surprised if your local law library has little information about the laws and court decisions made 'over the border'. Electronic databases have gone some way to removing this barrier to information flow, but if, for example, you are based in England and seeking details of Greek property legislation, or Portuguese employment law, the paper sources in England are sparse and the electronic non-existent. And if, as I have sometimes experienced, your enquirer wants the answer as an authoritative English summary ... !!!

2.4 Legal systems

Those jurisdictions that trace their law back to the Romans form the Civilian or Civil law system. The members comprise many of the countries of Western Europe, Latin America, as well as Quebec and Louisiana. Today their law is mostly contained in codes produced in the nineteenth century and amended from time to time. The code is the definitive source of law and the courts interpret the code to a particular situation; in some countries the courts are expressly forbidden to refer to earlier court decisions.

By contrast, in the Common law system, the legislature passes a steady stream of statutes that are applied by the courts to particular situations. In some areas of law there are no statutes and the courts have developed a body of decisions that form the law. The two sources of law: the statutes and the decisions of the courts, are of far more equal status than in the Civil law system. Consequently, the information base in Common law jurisdictions is extensive. The members of the Common law system include the United Kingdom, many Commonwealth countries and the United States.

Members of the Socialist legal system include the countries of Eastern Europe and the former Soviet Union, Cuba and China. The laws of these countries are based on written constitutions with laws made by an elected assembly that meets for only a few days a year. The decisions of the courts are not recognised as creating law.

Implications for LIS staff:

- don't expect to find the same types of law publication or terminology as those used in your own country, in countries with a different legal tradition

- within the same legal family (such as the Common law family including Britain and the United States) there will be similarities. Although the roots of the legal systems may be the same, over the centuries the law has developed in quite different ways, with different publications, different terminology and different approaches to researching the law.

2.5 Keeping up to date

Some publications print the text of a piece of legislation but have no means of informing the user that the legislation may have been amended or even repealed (revoked) by later legislation. Similarly, publications containing the text of the decisions of the courts usually do not indicate whether a particular decision has been overtaken by a later decision and is therefore no longer 'good law'. Law publishers have devised the loose-leaf format to overcome these difficulties. Many of the most valuable and comprehensive textbooks and encyclopaedias of law are now published wholly or partly in loose-leaf format. Substituting out-of-date pages in the binder for pages of text, regularly delivered, setting out new legal developments, is one of the more tedious aspects of law librarianship. If the insertion instructions are not adequate it can be frustrating also! Some publishers are starting to issue major law encyclopaedias in electronic form, with similar or better currency than the paper equivalents.

Implication for LIS staff:

- When researching legal information in paper format, use a publication with a loose-leaf format. A hardback could be years out of date. Always check the title page or the preface for a statement about the date up to which the law in the volume is correct.

- Then, carry out further research in other sources to bring the law up to date. If this is not possible make clear to whoever is asking for the information that what you are providing is information 'correct to' a particular date, which may not reflect the current situation.

In recent years computerised information retrieval services have made possible daily, and even more frequent updating. But the most frequently updated services are only indexes to the law. Lawyers want the law itself, so full-text services are popular. Full-text electronic services do not come cheaply, and the user has to apply search techniques quite different to index searching. In most circumstances it is good practice to research paper sources prior to going on-line, to become familiar with the major Acts or decisions, so that the on-line search is quick, efficient and effective.

2.6 Unpublished material

The natural assumption is that all the law made by the legislature and the courts of a country will be published and readily accessible to the public. In some Common law jurisdictions, such as the United Kingdom this is not so. For example, in England and Wales the courts hear and decide over 200,000 cases each year, but only about 2,500 (or 1.25%) are published, or as lawyers say, reported. Only those cases that develop the law, setting new precedents, are reported. The rest remain either as unpublished (unreported) transcripts or go totally unrecorded.

The situation is similar in the United States, but for a different reason. So many cases were being reported in the 1970s and 1980s that some States decided that the court should rule at the end of each case whether the transcript should be published. Only those decisions that create new precedent would be authorised by the court to be made publicly available.

Although electronic databases, such as LEXIS, carry the full text of a selection of unreported decisions of the higher English courts, reports of decisions made in the vast majority of English cases are not publicly available.

Implications for LIS staff:

- regardless of the jurisdiction, don't assume all court decisions are readily available in either printed or electronic form;
- information about cases decided in the lower courts of Common law jurisdictions may be difficult or even impossible to obtain.

2.7 Abbreviations and citations

The most comprehensive index to legal abbreviations is the *Index to Legal Citations and Abbreviations* by Donald Raistrick (London: Bowker-Saur, 2nd ed., 1993). The index covers not only abbreviations for law materials used in the United Kingdom and Ireland, but also the Commonwealth, the United States of America, member countries of the European Communities, other European countries, Africa, Asia and South America. Some legal abbreviations can refer to several quite different documents. For example, the abbreviation W.L.R. has entries referring to six different publications, one English, four US and one Canadian. A tip so as to avoid 'translating' the abbreviation you are checking into the wrong document and wasting time, is to choose the title of the document(s) published for the jurisdiction in which you are interested, then check that the publication dates given in the index are comparable with the ones you have. If they aren't, you may require one of the other documents listed against the abbreviation.

There are other lists that provide more details for the 'home' jurisdiction, but fewer entries than Raistrick for other jurisdictions. They are:

For the United Kingdom and European Communities:

Osborne, P. *Concise Law Dictionary*. (London: Sweet & Maxwell, 8th ed., 1993).

Current Law Case Citator. (London: Sweet & Maxwell, updated volume published annually).

Halsbury's Laws of England. (London: Butterworths, 4th ed., reissue, 1989). Volume 1 has a list at the front.

Sweet & Maxwell's Guide to Law Reports and Statutes. (London: Sweet & Maxwell, 4th ed., 1962). Covers English, Scots and Irish abbreviations and is good for older material.

For Ireland:

O'Malley, Thomas. *Sources of Law.* (Dublin: Round Hall Press. 1993). A brief list in Appendix 2. The author also refers users to the UK sources and some of the US sources mentioned here.

For Australia:

Fong, Colin & Edwards, Alan. *Australian and New Zealand Legal Abbreviations.* (Australian Law Librarians Group (New South Wales Branch) 1988).

Campbell, Enid. *Legal Research: Materials and Methods.* (Sydney: The Law Book Co., 3rd edition, 1988).

For Canada:

Banks, Margaret & Foti, Karen E.H. *Banks on Using a Law Library.* (Toronto: Carswell, 6th edition, 1994). Detailed lists in Appendices 2 & 3.

For the United States:

Black's Law Dictionary. (St. Paul, Minnesota: West Publishing Co., 6th ed., 1990). List at the back.

Index to Legal Periodicals and Books. (Bronx, N.Y.: H.W.Wilson Co., 11 issues per year). List at front of each issue.

Jacobstein, J. Myron & Mersky, Roy M. *Fundamentals of Legal Research.* (Westbury, N.Y.: Foundation Press. 1990). List at the back.

Price, M. O. & Bitner, H. *Effective Legal Research.* (Boston, Mass.: Little, Brown & Co., 3rd ed., 1969). Appendix III. The 1953 edition has an even fuller list, which is good for obscure, old, material.

3. The literature of law: British Isles

3.1 Types of law material

Generally speaking, the literature of the law of a jurisdiction comprises primary and secondary legal materials - as shown in figure 1.

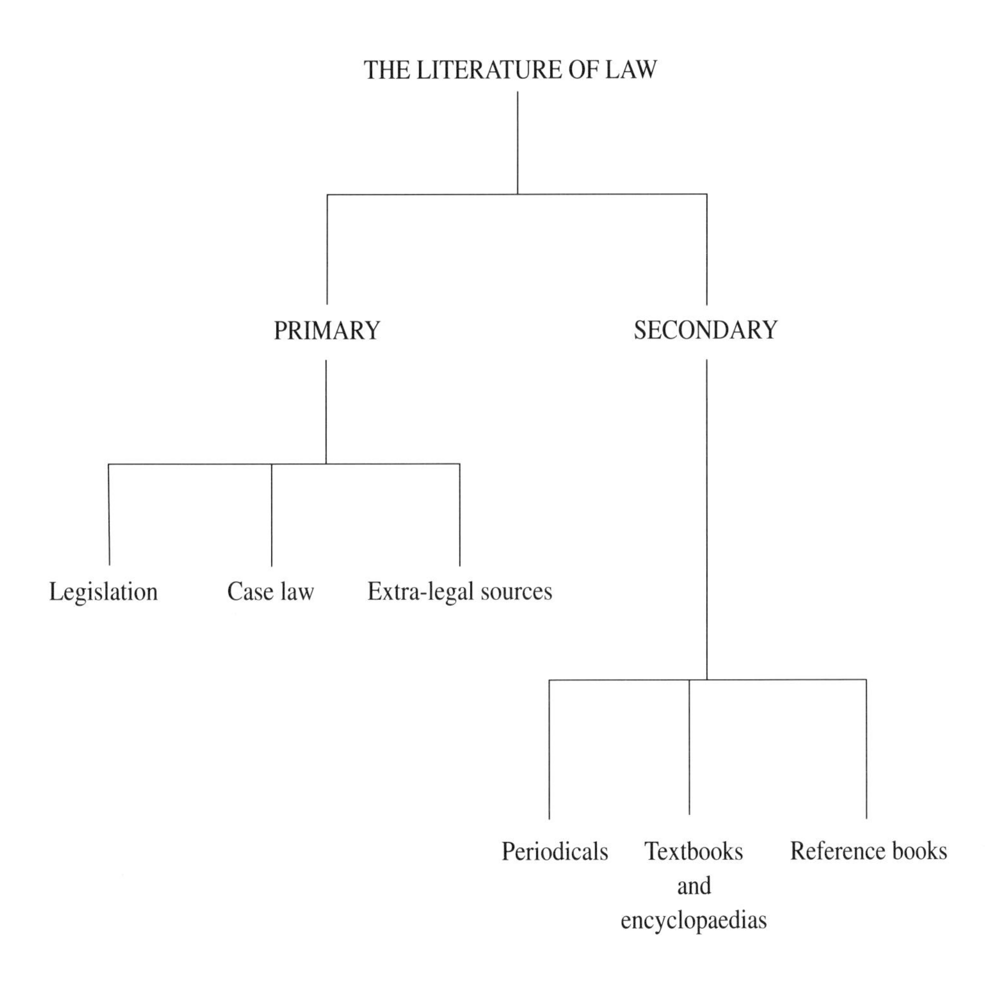

Figure 1 - Generalised diagram of the literature of the law for a Common law jurisdiction

The primary materials are the statement of the law itself, and the secondary are commentary, discussion and opinion on the primary. The primary frequently consist of two categories of material: legislation (the law made by the legislature or Parliament), and the decisions of the courts of law: case or judge-made law. There is sometimes a third category of primary material: codes, principles and standards of practice, possibly approved by bodies outside the legislature, Parliament or courts, which (whilst not having the force of law) are recognised as guides to good practice. The secondary materials comprise periodicals, textbooks, encyclopaedias and reference works. In the pages which follow a description of these types of legal material is organised according to jurisdiction.

3.2 England and Wales

In this section the major sources of the law of England and Wales will be discussed, starting with legislation, followed by case law, extra-legal sources and, finally, secondary sources. Figure 2 shows the relationship between and terminology used in English law for the sources of legislation.

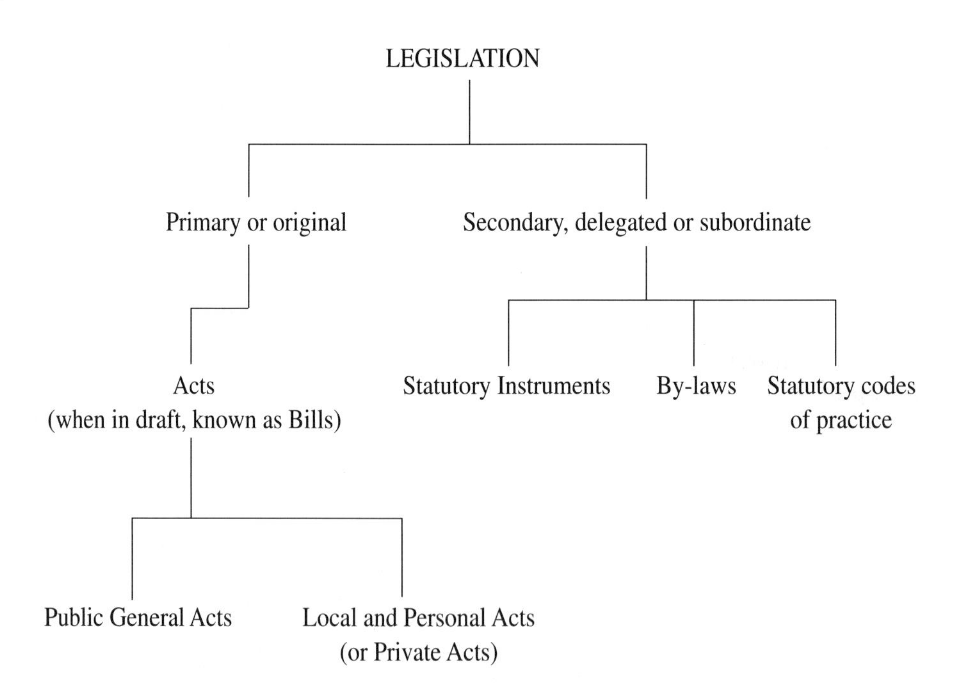

Figure 2 - The major source documents for the legislation of England and Wales

Legislation splits into two types: Primary or original and Secondary or delegated or subordinate. Broadly speaking, Primary or original legislation contains general principles agreed in Parliament, often only after considerable discussion and debate, whilst Secondary legislation comprises regulations for the detailed implementation of the agreed principles. Although also placed before Parliament for approval, only occasionally does secondary legislation create heated debate!

3.2.1 Acts

Description
The most common forms of UK Primary legislation are Acts of Parliament also known collectively as the statutes. In their draft form, before they have been approved by Parliament and received the Royal Assent, Acts are known as Bills of Parliament. There are two types of Act of Parliament: Public General Acts containing matters of public policy and which are of general application, and Local and Personal Acts (sometimes referred to as Private Acts). These latter give special powers to organisations or individuals, such as local authorities or public corporations.

Both types of Act are published by Her Majesty's Stationery Office (HMSO). They are issued within a short time of the Act receiving the Royal Assent. An Act is usually referred to by its short title, given at the head of the Act. As each Act is given the Royal Assent it forms a new chapter on the statute book for the year. The year and chapter number are printed under the short title and are a common shorthand way of referring to a particular Act. For example, the Child Support Act 1991, under which the Child Support Agency derives many of its powers, may be referred to as 1991 c. 48 (the 48th Act to receive the Royal Assent in 1991). The abbreviations chap. or ch. are also used for the word chapter.

Each Act is sub-divided into sections. The word section is frequently abbreviated in writing to 's' or, in the plural, 'ss'. Most modern Acts end with a group of sections which are of special value in legal research: amongst other matters they deal with the commencement (when the Act is to come into force) and the extent (detailing the geographical area to which the Act applies (see the note on jurisdiction in 2.3, above). Frequently the precise day on which an Act is to come into force will not be specified in the Act, but power is delegated to a Government Minister to set a date for commencement - an 'appointed day'. The Ministerial power is exercised through the issue of a 'commencement order', which is one of the several types of statutory instrument, discussed below. The commencement of an Act may be considerably delayed - whole Acts and sections of Acts given the Royal Assent in the 1970s and 1980s have yet to be brought into force. The reasons may be insufficient political will or administrative or financial cost.

3.2.1.1 Implications for LIS staff

- never assume that because an Act exists that it is in force
- always check the extent section at the end of an Act to see that it applies to the jurisdiction in which you are interested.

How do you ensure that the Act you have found is good law? See the section on answering queries below.

Public General Acts and Local and Personal Acts are published by HMSO. A number of official and unofficial collected editions of Public General Acts are widely available in law libraries and general academic and public libraries. Local and Personal Acts are much less widely available. A few academic law libraries collect them, and major public libraries or county record offices will collect the Local Acts relating to the geographical area they serve. In addition, since 1992, Local and Personal Acts have been reprinted in *Current Law Statutes Annotated,* which will be found in most law libraries.

3.2.1.2 Using Acts

The Paper Sources
The official versions of Public General Acts are published as loose issues and, at the end of each calendar year, in bound volumes entitled: *Public General Acts and General Synod Measures.* These volumes contain the Acts in the form in which they received the Royal Assent. *No* subsequent repeals or amendments are included. Although HMSO publishes updating services and subject indexes to the statutes, their appearance is so delayed you are advised NOT to refer to them. In fact, HMSO has suspended part of the publication of Statutes in Force because it has become so much delayed, and because work has commenced on an electronic version - Statute Law Database. At the date of writing, the electronic version is at the development stage. It will contain the full text of all *Public General Acts and General Synod Measures* (current and historical) and Local and Personal Acts currently in force. It will not be available to end users until 1997. Until then, commercially published versions of Acts of Parliament are to be preferred for better currency, wide availability and ease of use.

A helpful guide to library holdings of the official texts of Acts is given in *Parliamentary Holdings in Libraries in Britain and Ireland* by David Lewis Jones and Chris Pond (Westminster: House of Commons Library, 1993).

The two commercially published versions which you will probably find of most use are, firstly, *Current Law Statutes Annotated* and the associated *Current Law Statute and Legislation Citators,* published by Sweet & Maxwell and, secondly, *Halsbury's Statutes of England,* published by Butterworths. To use either set of publications properly requires a little practice. Explanatory booklets have been produced by both publishers. In addition Butterworths have produced a useful, single laminated sheet with the steps set out in diagrammatic form. Detailed instructions on how to use both publications are also given in *Using a Law Library* by Peter Clinch (London: Blackstone Press, 1992), subsequently referred to as Clinch (1992).

Which commercial publications should you use and when?

Current Law Statutes Annotated (CLSA) and its associated Citators are good for:

- researching the reasons why a particular Act became law
- tracing if an Act has been amended or repealed or if the courts have considered the meaning of any sections of the Act.

To use CLSA effectively you need to know the title of the Act relevant to your query. A subject search of CLSA and the Citators for Acts on a topic is not possible. CLSA reprints Acts of Parliament in annual volumes in the form and in the order in which they received the Royal Assent, with copious notes and annotations explaining the background to the Act. References are given to publications which influenced the legislation, such as Government reports, policy documents, notable decisions of the courts etc. Details are also given of where the verbatim reports of debates in Parliament on the Bill - the Act in draft - will be found in *Hansard.* Any changes to the Act or cases in which the wording of the Act has been considered by the courts, are listed in the accompanying Citators.

Halsbury's Statutes is good for tracing legislation in force at the present time on a subject or topic. *Halsbury's Statutes* reprints in over 50 volumes only those Acts or parts of Acts in force at the time of publication, but it does so in subject groups. It also has a very detailed subject index and an index arranged by the short titles of Acts. It is regularly updated. The commentary and annotations in *Halsbury's Statutes* are frequently briefer than in CLSA, but *Halsbury's* should be used if you have a subject query and no idea of which Act is relevant.

The Electronic Sources

There are two key sources: Lawtel and LEXIS. Lawtel is a digest of information, containing summaries of Acts. It is up-dated daily. It is best used for current awareness. LEXIS, on the other hand, contains the full text of all Public General Acts currently in force in England and Wales. The database is held on a computer in Dayton, Ohio, USA. It is updated each week, but it may take several weeks between the publication of the HMSO copy of a new Act and its inclusion in the database, especially if it is a major piece of legislation effecting many changes to existing law; nevertheless, the database is reasonably up to date. The text of every Act on LEXIS includes amendments made by subsequent legislation; the text is not merely a reprint of the Act in the form in which it received the Royal Assent. Access to LEXIS is available to subscribers; more details are provided in chapter 5.

3.2.1.3 Answering queries

- Is this Public General Act in force? Has any part of it been amended or repealed by subsequent legislation?

Either use the electronic databases: LEXIS or Lawtel, but note that Lawtel currently contains details for statutes passed since 1 January 1984 only; or use *Current Law Statute* and *Legislation Citators* or *Halsbury's Statutes.*

- Tracing Acts currently in force by subject

Either use the electronic databases: LEXIS or Lawtel. Since LEXIS is a full text database care will need to be taken in selecting the most appropriate search terms. For Lawtel it is necessary to note that the database contains details back to 1 January 1984 only; or use *Halsbury's Statutes.*

- Are there any cases on this Act or section of an Act?

Either use the electronic databases LEXIS or Lawtel; or *Current Law Statute* and *Legislation Citators* or *Halsbury's Statutes.*

3.2.2 Secondary legislation

There are a number of different types of secondary legislation: statutory instruments, by-laws and statutory codes of practice.

Statutory instruments
The term 'statutory instrument' (often abbreviated to SI) was introduced in the Statutory Instruments Act 1946. SIs are secondary legislation made by a Minister and approved by Parliament or made by the Queen in Council. Prior to that date these documents were called statutory rules and orders (SR&O); some are still in force. Individual statutory instruments are entitled 'regulations' 'rules', 'orders', 'warrants', or 'schemes'. Although users of the instruments will refer to them by their individual titles, in the law library you will not find separate collections entitled 'regulations' or 'rules' and so on, but volumes under the generic name: statutory instruments. There are two broad classes of statutory instrument: general or local. The distinction is analogous to that between a Public General Act and a Local and Personal Act. General instruments are published and sold by HMSO, several separate instruments appearing each working day (several thousand are published each year). They are often referred to in a shorthand way, by citing only the letters SI, then the year, followed by a slash '/' and then a running number (e.g. SI 1989/1674).

Even with this sparse information it is easy to find a copy of the instrument through the publications and databases noted in sections 3.2.2.1 and 3.2.2.2 below. Local instruments are exempt from printing and sale unless the Minister concerned requests otherwise. The difficulties in tracing local instruments, and lots of helpful information on how to overcome them, are discussed in an article by R.J.B Morris: Finding and using local statutory instruments. (1990, 11 *Statute Law Review* 28).

By-laws
By-laws are secondary legislation made by a local or public authority (such as the British Waterways Board) under powers given by an Act of Parliament. By the Local Government Act 1972 (s.236) local authority by-laws must be available for inspection at the offices of the local authority by whom the by-laws were made, and the by-laws should be available for sale to the public. By-laws of other bodies are likely to be available for inspection or purchase at their offices. Libraries are unlikely to collect by-laws, except that the larger public libraries may keep by-laws relating to the local authority in whose area they are located.

Statutory codes of practice
There is no official definition for these. The oldest, and certainly the most well known, is the Highway Code, first devised in the 1930s. A large number of codes have been drawn up since the 1970s under powers given to a Minister or other official body to lay down guidance or provide a statement of good practice. Some do have legal effect and may be used in the courts to establish or negate liability. Unfortunately, there is no common practice about publishing statutory codes. Many, like the Highway Code, are published by HMSO; some, like the codes prepared by the Equal Opportunities Commission for the elimination of discrimination in employment, are published by the organisation which prepared them. The best source to use when tracing the text of a particular code is a loose-leaf law encyclopaedia covering the subject. For example, a number of codes of practice relating to industrial relations law are reprinted complete with, in some cases, the addition of footnotes by the encyclopaedia editors, in the following specialist titles:

- *Encyclopaedia of Labour Relations Law* (published by Sweet & Maxwell)
- *Encyclopaedia of Employment Law and Practice* (published by Professional Publishing).

In addition, a textbook published in loose-leaf format: *Harvey on Industrial Relations and Employment Law* (published by Butterworths) includes several codes.

3.2.2.1 Using secondary legislation

Paper sources

As was noted above, several statutory instruments are published each day. At the end of each calendar year, annual volumes entitled *Statutory Instruments,* containing reprints of general instruments, are published by HMSO. Unfortunately, publication is frequently delayed by several years. The SIs are arranged in running number order and there is a subject index at the back of the final volume published for each year. HMSO does publish subject indexes and chronological (i.e. running number) indexes to SIs but they are not kept so up to date nor are they so easy to use as commercially published versions. The Statute Law Database project run by the Statutory Publications Office aims to include the full text of all general instruments published since 1991, and the full text of selected instruments from before that date. The database is not due to be available before 1997.

A helpful guide to library holdings of the official texts of SIs is given in *Parliamentary Holdings in Libraries in Britain and Ireland* by David Lewis Jones and Chris Pond (Westminster: House of Commons Library, 1993).

Halsbury's Statutory Instruments (published by Butterworths) is one of the best places to start when researching SIs. It is updated each month and has very detailed subject, title and chronological indexes. Unfortunately, it does not reprint all SIs and provides only summaries of many. However, because of its superior indexing and currency Halsbury's SIs is the best place to start your research in every instance, except:

- where you have already the year and running number of the SI you want, in which case, you can go straight to the HMSO publications, because they are arranged in that order

- when you are looking for an SI which was issued during the last few weeks, and may not have been published in Halsbury's yet, in which case go to the HMSO individual loose issues.

To use *Halsbury's* SIs correctly takes a little practice. Butterworths, the publishers, have provided a users' booklet with the encyclopaedia and a single, laminated sheet with diagrammatic instructions. Detailed instructions on how to use the publication are also given in Clinch (1992) (see page 13).

Electronic sources

There are three key sources: LEXIS, Lawtel and the JUSTIS SI-CD (Statutory Instruments CD-ROM) produced by Context Ltd.

LEXIS contains the full text of all general SIs currently in force in England and Wales. The database is updated each week but it sometimes takes a while for new SIs to be added. The text of every SI on LEXIS includes any subsequent amendments and is not just a reprint of the SI in the form in which it was originally approved by Parliament.

Lawtel is an on-line digest of legal information. It does not include the text of SIs but only certain information about them. The database is updated daily, so is best used for current awareness or to trace very recent instruments.

JUSTIS SI-CD is published in co-operation with HMSO and contains the full text of SIs published by HMSO since 1 January 1987, with short form references to SIs published between 1980 and 1987. It is possible to search on any word, rather like on LEXIS. But there are two drawbacks:

- the discs are updated at six monthly intervals so it is not possible to search for recent SIs, although registered users can gain access to the JUSTIS ONLINE updating service
- for technical reasons, anything in an SI set out in tabular form is not included on the disc.

3.2.2.2 Answering queries

- You know the title of an SI but not the year or running number. How do you trace it?

Amongst the paper sources start with the appropriate index to *Halsbury's* SIs and if the SI is not printed in full in that publication, go to the HMSO version. If you wish to use electronic sources, in SI-CD you can search the 'heading' field, but note the limited date range of the database. Lawtel may be used but again the date range is limited. LEXIS may be used, but as with all the databases, because there are so many SIs issued each year, some with very similar titles, care should be taken to ensure any SI you find is the one relevant to your research.

- Is this SI still in force?

For a paper search start with the appropriate index to *Halsbury's* SIs making sure that you end the search by checking the annual and monthly surveys which cover recent developments. To bridge the gap between the compilation of *Halsbury's* and the present, a search will be necessary of either the recent individual HMSO issues or HMSO *Daily List*. The *Daily List* is a catalogue of the publications made available by HMSO that day, and is available in printed or electronic form. Most law libraries and large public libraries will subscribe to it. Of the electronic sources, use of SI-CD is not recommended because of its poor currency as compared with other products unless you use the JUSTIS ONLINE updating service. Lawtel will provide the most up to date information but only as a summary; LEXIS, on the other hand, includes only the text of SIs currently in force.

- Has this SI been amended?

Halsbury's SIs will provide an answer to this question but, for completeness, a search of HMSO SIs published in the last month or so, will be needed to bridge the gap between compilation of *Halsbury's* and the present. SI-CD is not an appropriate source because it reproduces SIs in their original form and does not indicate amendments. On the other hand, LEXIS contains the text of SIs as amended. Lawtel is up to date, but can only provide a summary of the SI.

3.2.3 Case law

Case law comprises the reports of the decisions of the courts. In contrast to Acts and Statutory Instruments, case law is a rather more difficult type of law material to research. There are two reasons for this:

- there is no official series of law reports in this jurisdiction - there is no official, authentic record of what the courts have determined in every case. Traditionally, law reporting has been in private hands, and although HMSO publishes a number of specialised series of law reports - on tax, immigration and social security matters - the great majority of reports are published by many different, often competing, private publishers

- whilst the courts hear and decide over 200,000 cases each year only about 2,500 (or 1.25%) are published or as lawyers say, reported. The rest remain as unpublished (unreported) transcripts or go totally unrecorded.

3.2.3.1 Implications for LIS staff

- there can be several different versions of the same case published in different series of law reports. Which should you choose?

- you may be asked to find a report of a case that has not been reported (published). How do you trace where it might be obtained?

Different types of law report
Law reports may be divided into four types; Table 1 shows their relationship one to another.

	Advance	**Full-text**
General (all subjects)	All subjects Edited reports	All subjects Full reports
Specialist (selected subjects)	Selected subjects Edited reports	Selected subjects Full reports

Table 1 - Typology of modern law reports

The general series attempt to report cases on points of law of wide interest, and the specialist series select cases of particular interest to lawyers working in a discrete practice area, i.e. specific field of legal activity. These two categories of reports may be divided into firstly, the 'advance reports' - using United States terminology - being those reports of judgements which are published in brief, edited form, but issued as rapidly as possible and, secondly, the full-text reports which report judgements verbatim but are subject to some delay. Amongst the general 'advance' series are the law reports found in the quality daily newspapers, such as *The Times, Financial Times, Guardian* and *Independent.* Two other generalist publications: the *Weekly Law Reports* and the *All England Law Reports* normally publish full-text reports but often after some months delay. A similar pattern will be found amongst the specialist series: for example, the *Criminal Law Review* publishes brief reports of cases after a short delay, while *Criminal Appeal Reports* prints full-text cases much later. Unfortunately, it does not follow that a case reported briefly will be reported fully at a later date. Some cases are reported only in the newspapers and never in the full-text reports. If there is a choice between different reports of a case, lawyers prefer the fullest available.

Mention has been made of the quality newspapers as a source for reports of cases. A very important point to remember is that lawyers and law libraries are interested in collecting reports of cases which create new precedent - decisions which extend, modify or clarify the law. They are not concerned with journalistic reports of controversial or notorious cases in topics such as murder, divorce, defamation (libel and slander) or the award of large sums as damages which, although creating considerable public interest, rarely create new precedent. For example, there is no published law report of the James Bulger case, in which a toddler was abducted and murdered by two young boys. A transcript is available - at a price - from the firm of shorthand writers who attended the proceedings, but no readily available report exists. The circumstances of the death were horrific but the case did not establish new legal precedent.

Tracing unreported cases

The selection of cases for publication is left to private enterprise - the editors of the various law report publications. The operation of the principle of precedent relies on an hierarchical arrangement of the courts. It is generally true that the higher the court in the hierarchy the greater the likelihood of its decisions being reported. In practice virtually every report of the House of Lords is reported, and a large number of the Court of Appeal (Civil Division). But at the High Court level, only around a fifth to a third of the decisions of the constituent courts, the Family and Chancery Divisions and Queen's Bench, are published. Only about 10% of the decisions of the Court of Appeal (Criminal Division) are reported. Many cases are heard by tribunals (such as social welfare, industrial relations, landlord and tenant, immigration and VAT) but only a handful are reported. At Crown Court and County Court level only about 1 or 2 in every 10,000 are reported.

LEXIS, the computer database, contains the transcripts of unreported cases made since 1 January 1980, from the House of Lords, Privy Council, and Court of Appeal (Civil Division), along with selected decisions of the High Court and some tribunals. As for those cases not on LEXIS, the Lord Chancellor's Department Library Services has produced a very useful free booklet entitled *'Supreme Court Library Transcripts - What is available and how to obtain them'* which gives addresses, telephone and fax numbers of those responsible for transcripts at all levels of court. A similar list appears in *Butterworths Legal Research Guide* by Guy Holborn (London: Butterworths, 1993) in the Quick Reference Section at para QR4.16. Its worth noting that no formal record of Magistrates' Courts proceedings is kept, and that for Crown and County Courts, the courts themselves should be contacted.

3.2.3.2 Citation of law reports

If a decision is published it is likely to be referred to in a shorthand way:

> Rolled Steel Products Ltd v BSC [1985] 3 All ER 52

This legal citation means that the case will be found in the All England Law Reports for 1985, volume 3 at page 52. Lists of the most frequently used abbreviations for law reports are given in:

> Raistrick, D. *Index to Legal Citations and Abbreviations* (London: Bowker-Saur, 2nd. ed., 1993)
>
> The first volume of *Halsbury's Laws of England* (London: Butterworths)
>
> Any issue of *Current Law Monthly Digest, Current Law Yearbook* or *Current Law Case Citator* (all Sweet & Maxwell)
>
> Osborn, P. *Concise Law Dictionary* (London: Sweet & Maxwell, 8th. ed., 1993)

3.2.3.3 Using case law

There are five different types of database or publication which will help you find cases:

- full text reports of the cases themselves
- indexes to law reports
- indexes with brief summaries of cases
- citators
- commentaries on the law relating different case decisions to each other.

Full text reports of the cases themselves
Most law libraries will have sets of the general series of law reports, such as the *All England Law Reports,* the *Weekly Law Reports, The Law Reports* and the law reports appearing in some of the daily newspapers *(The Times, The Financial Times, Guardian, Independent).* The range of specialist reports held will depend on the needs of the library's users. LEXIS, the on-line database, contains the full text of all cases reported since 1945 and a large number of unreported cases of the Court of Appeal (Civil Division), some from the High Court and selected tribunals. Link (Legal Information Network), an on-line information system aimed primarily at practising lawyers, has about 5,000 full text transcripts of cases heard in the Court of Appeal (Civil Division) and House of Lords since 1993. JUSTIS ONLINE is a database containing the full text of reports appearing in the *Weekly Law Reports* (January 1981 to date), the *Independent* (October 1987 to date) and *The Times* (December 1989 to date), as well as indexes to other law reports. It is updated weekly. JUSTIS WEEKLY LAW CD contains the same material as JUSTIS ONLINE but back to 1971and is updated twice a year. Context, the publishers of the JUSTIS products are pioneering the combination of on-line and CD technology in the law field.

LEXIS is by far the most comprehensive case law source. It is available to subscribers. Link is a relatively new service which is largely free to search but charges are made for downloading information. Further details about LEXIS and Link are provided in chapter 5. The JUSTIS databases are valuable but both are restricted by the limited number of report titles included.

Indexes to law reports
One series of law reports entitled *The Law Reports* publishes a set of red or pink coloured volumes which is an index to that series and about eight others. *Legal Journals Index,* first published in 1986 as a paper database and now available electronically, indexes the contents of over 200 law periodicals published in the United Kingdom, including journals which carry brief reports of cases on a wide range of general and specialist topics.

Indexes with brief summaries of cases
Daily Law Reports Index started in 1988 as a paper publication and is now available electronically. It indexes the 1,500 or so cases reported annually in the daily newspapers. *Current Law Monthly Digest* commenced in 1947 and

provides a monthly digest or summary of changes in the law. Summaries of new cases are arranged under broad subject headings. Lawtel is an on-line digest of legal information containing summaries of cases. The database commenced in January 1980, and new cases are added as soon as the newspaper report or transcript is to hand. When a case is printed in the law reports Lawtel adds details of those citations.

Citators
Current Law Case Citator is invaluable for tracing where a case is reported when you do not have the full citation. The *Citator* is a list, arranged alphabetically by case name, of all reported cases published since 1947. Each entry gives details of where the case is published. In many instances more than one citation is given, since a case can be published in several different law report publications. If there is a choice, lawyers prefer to use the longest version available, so choose a report in one of the full text sources. The *Citator* is published in several volumes, each covering a different time period. The most recent cases are listed in the case index at the back of the latest issue of *Current Law Monthly Digest.*

Commentaries on the law relating different case decisions to each other
Halsbury's Law of England is a key research publication. It is a commentary, written by the editorial staff of Butterworths, on the whole law of England and Wales. Copious footnotes give citations to cases and statutes on points of law. It is one of the best places to start if you wish to find cases on a subject or relate the decisions in a number of cases to one another. The publishers provide a user's guide with the publication and also a single, laminated sheet with instructions in diagrammatic form. More detailed instructions may be found in Clinch (1992), (see page 13).

You are likely to find most, if not all, of these publications in a law library. Public libraries rarely subscribe to law reports but you may find *Halsbury's Laws of England* available.

3.2.3.4 Answering queries

- Tracing the report of a case where only the names of parties are known

Probably the first publication to turn to will be *Current Law Case Citator.* As an alternative, *Law Reports Index* or the consolidated tables and index to the *All England Law Reports* will help. If you suspect that the case has been very recently decided then *Daily Law Reports Index* and *Legal Journals Index* should be used. Lawtel and LEXIS may be used for this research but, because of cost, the latter is best not searched until the paper sources have been exhausted.

- Has this case been considered by the courts on a subsequent occasion?

Because of their comprehensive coverage there are really only two sources to use for this research: either LEXIS or *Current Law Case Citator.* With the latter publication, it is necessary first to find the entry for the case in which you are interested, then to note any references to a sister publication: *Current Law Yearbook,* in which summaries of decisions are printed. The references to these summaries are listed at the end of each entry in the *Citator,* preceded by the word 'Digested'. The numbers denote the year of *Current Law Yearbook* and paragraph number at which the summary is printed. Once you have found the reference to the case in which you are interested, continue your search through the more recent issues of the *Citator* to check how the courts have viewed the original decision in later cases. Look out for any indication that the original case has been 'overruled' or 'not followed' in a later decision. Follow up these references in *Current Law Year Book,* for they indicate that the original decision may no longer be 'good law'. Instructions on how to use the *Citators* and *Year Books* may be found in Clinch (1992), (see page 13).

- Tracing cases on a subject

LEXIS and Lawtel are appropriate databases for this research, but note the more restricted time period covered by Lawtel. Amongst the paper sources, *Halsbury's Laws* is pre-eminent.

- Have there been any case notes or articles on this case, which will help me to understand its meaning and effect?

Legal Journals Index is probably the best source to use because it indexes such a wide range of journals and it is reasonably current - only two or three weeks delay in the on-line electronic version. LEXIS has the full text of a small selection of law journals and may be useful. Link carries the full text of articles from a range of practitioner publications - the ones that solicitors and barristers rather than university or college lecturers are likely to use. Amongst the paper sources, *Current Law Monthly Digest* and *Current Law Yearbook* have indexes to journal articles but they are not arranged by case name, so searching is awkward.

3.2.4 Extra-legal sources

These comprise a wide range of documents variously called codes of practice, codes of conduct, guidance or standards. They differ from those discussed above in two ways:

- any organisation can issue them, whereas statutory codes can only be issued under powers conferred by legislation
- extra-legal sources are not legally enforceable in their own right, but seek to influence behaviour or advise or ensure conformity of practice.

Here are just three organisations and the extra-legal sources they produce.

First, the British Standards Institution, which has a current catalogue of over 10,000 British Standards with more than 700 new or revised standards issued each year. The aim of the publications is to set generally recognised standards of quality for industry and commerce. The familiar 'kitemark' on a product, followed by a British Standard number (normally abbreviated to BS followed by a running number) indicates that the product or service satisfies the requirements of that standard.

Second, the Fair Trading Act 1973 placed a duty on the Director General of Fair Trading to encourage the preparation of Codes of Practice by trade associations. Nearly 30 have been produced. They state the legal responsibilities of traders supporting them and the benefits consumers may receive in excess of their strict legal requirements. Examples of well known ones include the *Association of British Travel Agents Ltd. (ABTA) Tour Operators' Code of Conduct* and the *Code of Practice for the Motor Industry* covering advertising, sales, repair and servicing of both new and used cars.

Third, the Data Protection Act 1984 places a duty on the Data Protection Registrar to encourage trade associations to prepare and disseminate codes on compliance with the data protection principles enshrined in the Act.

Since any organisation can produce these types of document, each organisation responsible for a code or standard, will adopt its own policy on publication. Many university and large public libraries will have complete sets of the British Standards Institution publications, but other extra-legal sources may be hard to obtain. The best places to look are in specialist loose-leaf law encyclopaedias. For example, O'Keefe, J.A. *The law relating to Trade Descriptions* (London: Butterworths, loose-leaf) or Chalton, S.N.L. and Gaskill, S.J. *Encyclopedia of Data Protection* (London: Sweet & Maxwell, loose-leaf) cover the examples given in the previous paragraph.

3.2.5 Secondary sources

Textbooks

Law textbooks are a very useful starting point when trying to understand the meaning and effect of the major primary sources in an area of law. There are several categories of textbooks, ranging from practitioners' books, which provide a very detailed treatment of a subject and are usually read selectively, and used more as a reference work, to student textbooks, which are less concerned with detail but more with describing the general principles of law. There are also casebooks which reprint or summarise key cases and other law materials on a topic. Details of all these and other types of textbook such as practice books (not covered here) may be traced through the catalogues of the major law publishers in England & Wales such as Butterworths, Sweet & Maxwell and Blackstone Press (see chapter 5 for contact information). Valuable comprehensive listings of law textbooks are provided in the annual catalogues of two of the largest law booksellers in the UK: Hammick's Bookshop and Law Notes Bookshop (see chapter 5 for contact information). Details of recent law textbooks are given in *Current Law Monthly Digest,* in both the body of the *Digest* and as a list at the back of each issue. The standard general listings such as Bookfind, Bookbank and British National Bibliography may be used to trace law books on a topic.

Some law publishers are starting to produce texts in electronic format. In 1994 Butterworths launched Books on Screen in which selected paper texts were transferred into hypertext format, to enable users to search for information quickly, annotate the text with personal notes, and create bookmarks making it possible to quickly return on another occasion to a particular part of the text. Also, HMSO and CLS (UK) Ltd., have jointly developed hypertext versions of tax and VAT materials: HyperTax and HyperVAT.

Periodicals

To find commentary in law periodicals it is best to use one of the periodical indexing services now available. *Legal Journals Index,* established in September 1986, is the pre-eminent index in the English jurisdiction. It indexes over 200 journals and in its on-line electronic form is updated fortnightly. A CD version has just appeared but lacks the currency of the on-line version. *Current Law Monthly Digest* also indexes journal articles, but it is less easy to use and covers fewer source journals than *Legal Journals Index.* LEXIS has the full text of a small selection of law journals and is of limited use. Link carries the full text of articles from a range of practitioner publications.

There are a number of indexing services which cover law or law-related topics. *Criminology and Penology Abstracts* and *British Humanities Index.* The quality daily newspapers often carry commentary on legal topics. The paper copies supplemented by the newspaper CDs, such as *The Times, Guardian* and *Independent,* can be a valuable source.

Reference works

General law dictionaries include:

Mozley and Whiteley's Law Dictionary (London: Butterworths,10th ed., 1988)

A Concise Dictionary of Law (London: Sweet & Maxwell, 2nd ed., 1990)

Osborn's Law Dictionary (London: Sweet & Maxwell, 8th ed., 1993)

Jowitt's Dictionary of English Law (London: Sweet & Maxwell, 2nd ed., 1977) - in 2 volumes updated by supplements published every few years.

A Dictionary of Legal Quotations (London: Croom Helm, 1987)

Judicial Dictionaries

Stroud's Judicial Dictionary of Words and Phrases (London: Sweet & Maxwell, 5th ed., 1986) - in six volumes updated by occasional supplements: provide details of the interpretations by judges of words and phrases, as well as references to definitions included in statutes.

Words and Phrases Legally Defined (London: Butterworths, 3rd ed., 1988-9) in four volumes with annual supplements - similar to Stroud but provides verbatim extracts of speeches and judgements.

Biographical dictionaries

For those still living

Who's Who in the Law (London: Legalese, 1991) - biographies of about 2,000 eminent practising lawyers

Havers' Companion to the Bar (Canterbury: Havers Directories Ltd., Annual) -biographies of 4,000 individual barristers

For those deceased

Biographical Dictionary of the Common Law (London: Butterworths,1984)

Who was Who (London: A & C Black)

Dictionary of National Biography (Oxford: Oxford University Press)

Directories

Chambers & Partners' Directory. The top 1,000 Law Firms in England, Wales & Scotland and all Barristers' Chambers (London: Chambers & Partners Publishing, Annual) - invaluable guide arranged by legal; specialisation and geographical location.

Directory of Solicitors and Barristers (London: Law Society, Annual) - official listing.

The Bar Directory: The General Council of the Bar (London: Legalese, Annual) - official listing.

Hazell's Guide to the Judiciary and the Courts (Henley-on-Thames: R Hazell & Co, Annual)

Shaw's Directory of Courts in the United Kingdom (London: Shaw & Sons, Annual) - includes Scotland and Northern Ireland

Compendia

Oxford Companion to Law (Oxford: Clarendon Press, 1980) - thousands of dictionary-like entries on legal institutions, systems of law, legal ideas and principles of law.

Pritchard, John. *The New Penguin Guide to the Law* (London, Viking, 2nd ed., 1992) - highly readable lay person's guide to the law and the legal system of England and Wales.

It would also be helpful to look at a specialist classification scheme for law, e.g. *Moys Classification and Thesaurus for Legal Materials,* Elizabeth Moys, 3rd ed., Bowker Saur, London 1992, to see how the various aspects fit together.

Official publications
Apart from Bills of Parliament, Acts and Statutory Instruments, lawyers are interested in a number of other official publications. Command Papers or other important policy documents or Reports of Royal Commissions or other investigations undertaken outside Parliament. Some indicate Government thinking on future legislation or contain the recommendations of investigations on a matter of public concern. For example, the Royal Commission on Criminal Justice of July 1993 (Cm 2263) reported on the criminal justice system as a result of the quashing of the conviction for murder of the 'Birmingham Six' - the six men who had been convicted following the bomb explosions in public houses in Birmingham in November 1974, and who had in consequence served over 16 years in prison. Reports and consultative documents of a permanent organisation, the Law Commission, set up to keep the whole body of law under review, give details of proposals for changes in the law. They are published by HMSO. Some quasi-autonomous non-governmental organisations (quangos) such as the Equal Opportunities Commission and the Health and Safety Commission publish documents of value to lawyers, but they do so direct and not through HMSO. The best way to track these down is to use the Catalogue of British Official Publications Not Published by HMSO (Chadwyck-Healey) or its CD-ROM equivalent United Kingdom Official Publications (UKOP), which includes the HMSO Catalogue as well.

A helpful guide to library holdings of Parliamentary publications - which include Command Papers and Law Commission Reports - is given in *Parliamentary Holdings in Libraries in Britain and Ireland* by David Lewis Jones and Chris Pond (Westminster: House of Commons Library, 1993). The HMSO Annual Catalogue includes at the front a list of libraries in the UK with major collections of HMSO publications.

3.3 Scotland

The Scottish legal system is a 'mixed' system, influenced by both the neighbouring Common law system of England and Wales and the continental Civil law system. This explains why many of the basic principles of Scottish law are so different from English law. There are also differences in the legal profession and the structure of the courts. The study of Roman law is still an important element in Scottish legal education today.

Since 1707, when the English and Scottish Parliaments were united, the major forms of legislation have been the same as in England and Wales: Public General Acts and secondary legislation, mainly statutory instruments. It is very important for those using legislation in Scotland to be aware of the geographical extent of Acts of Parliament. Some will apply to the whole of the United Kingdom, some to Scotland only and in others only certain sections will apply to Scotland. Check the 'extent' section(s) printed towards the end of the Act for this information.

The modern official sources of Acts for Scotland published by HMSO are the same as for England and Wales. As to the commercially published versions, from 1991 *Current Law Statutes Annotated* has included the text of Scottish Acts. Prior to 1991 the text was included in a separate publication: *Scottish Current Law Statutes. Current Law Statute Citators* (London: Sweet & Maxwell) include information about Scottish statutes. There is no equivalent to *Halsbury's Statutes of England* covering the statutes of Scotland. However, *Is it in Force?,* a part of *Halsbury's Statutes of England,* does provide details of the dates of commencement, repeal and amendment of Scottish statutes. Statutes applying only to Scotland are not included on LEXIS.

As for secondary legislation, there are two types of statutory instrument peculiar to Scotland. Acts of Sederunt and Acts of Adjournal are procedural instruments published in a periodical: *Scots Law Times.* Those in force currently are collected in an updating publication entitled the *Parliament House Book* (London: Sweet & Maxwell). Other statutory instruments applying to Scotland will be found in the same sources noted for England and Wales (as described above), with the exception that there is no equivalent for Scotland of *Halsbury's Statutory Instruments.* Secondary legislation applying only to Scotland is not included on LEXIS.

Many of the points about the case law of England and Wales made above also apply to Scotland: the small proportion of cases which are published, the different types of law report publication, the way in which cases are cited by lawyers. When using a citator to check a case reference be sure to use the Scottish section of *Current Law Case Citator.* Also, when searching *Current Law Monthly Digest* remember that it is arranged by jurisdiction and the Scottish material is in a separate section of the publication. *Legal Journals Index* and *Daily Law Reports Index* both cover Scottish case law. An alerting service unique to Scotland is *Green's Weekly Digest,* which carries summaries of all the decisions received by the publishers, W. Green and Son, who also publish *Scottish Law Times.* The Scottish equivalent to *Halsbury's Laws of England* is *The Laws of Scotland: Stair Memorial Encyclopedia* (Edinburgh: Butterworths). When complete it will be a 27 volume encyclopaedia of annotated narrative of Scottish law arranged by subject, complete with updating service. LEXIS includes the full text of Scottish cases from 1950 onwards in the SCOT library (separate from English cases), and also unreported cases from several Scottish courts commencing at different dates in the 1980s.

Noting the above differences between English and Scottish legal information, it should be possible to follow the same research steps outlined for England and Wales above to answer enquiries.

There are two directories of Scottish lawyers: the long established *Scottish Law Directory* (Edinburgh: Law Society of Scotland), and new publication: *The Blue Book: the Directory of the Law Society of Scotland* (Edinburgh: Butterworths).

For further information on the main sources of Scottish law see: *Legal Research in Scotland,* Valerie Duffy, (Hebden Bridge: Legal Information Resources Ltd., 1992) or *How to use a Scottish Law Library,* Dawn Mackey, (Edinburgh: W Green 1992) or *Butterworths Legal Research Guide,* Guy Holborn, (London: Butterworths, 1993) or Dane and Thomas on *How to use a Law Library,* Cathie Cope and Philip A. Thomas. (London: Sweet & Maxwell, 3rd edition, 1995).

3.4 Northern Ireland

Up to 1801 there was a separate Parliament for the whole of Ireland. From that year until 1921 the United Kingdom Parliament in London legislated for the whole of Ireland. When the Government of Ireland Act 1920 came into effect the constitutional and legislative paths of Northern and Southern Ireland diverged. Since 1921 the complex constitutional arrangements in Northern Ireland have been reflected in the changing system for the creation and publication of legislation. Between 1921 and 1972 the Parliament of Northern Ireland (often referred to as 'Stormont') created legislation which was published by HMSO, Belfast. When the Parliament of Northern Ireland was dissolved in March 1972, the province came under direct rule from Westminster. Legislation applying to Northern Ireland was published as Orders in Council, a sub-set of the United Kingdom secondary legislation known as statutory instruments, published by HMSO, London (as described above). The new Northern Ireland Assembly lasted from July 1973 to May 1974 and during its life it passed four 'measures' which were published by HMSO, Belfast. Since 1974 government has reverted to direct rule from Westminster and the pattern of legislation is now as described above. At the time of writing there is no electronic database containing the statutes relating to Northern Ireland.

Statutes Revised, Northern Ireland, 2nd edition (HMSO) contains all legislation in force as at 31st March 1981, except for United Kingdom statutes passed at Westminster since 1922 which extend to, or apply only to, Northern Ireland. These exceptions will be found in the publications relating to England and Wales, such as the *Public General Acts and General Synod Measures and Current Law Statutes Annotated* (as described above). HMSO, Belfast issues annual cumulative supplements to *Statutes Revised, Northern Ireland,* but the text of the work itself has not been updated. As to secondary legislation, statutory instruments applying to Northern Ireland have been published singly since 1922 by HMSO, Belfast. They are later published in a bound volume publication: *Northern Ireland Statutory Rules and Orders,* again published by HMSO, Belfast. Again, at present, there is no electronic database containing Northern Ireland secondary legislation.

The 'official' law reports for Northern Ireland are the *Northern Ireland Law Reports* (Belfast: Incorporated Council of Law Reporting), but their publication is delayed. Since 1971 the *Northern Ireland Judgements Bulletin* (Belfast: Incorporated Council of Law Reporting) has provided 'advanced' reports of judgements. In other respects the Northern Ireland law reporting system is similar to that of England and Wales (as described above). LEXIS has a NILAW library containing the full text of general case law reported in the *Northern Ireland Law Reports* since 1945, and unreported cases beginning March 1984. The *Bulletin of Northern Ireland Law* (Belfast: SLS Legal Publications), begun in 1981 and published in ten parts a year, is a good updating service. *Current Law Monthly Digest* (London: Sweet & Maxwell) includes a section giving details of latest legal developments in Northern Ireland. The paper and electronic database: *Legal Journals Index* (Hebden Bridge: Legal Information Resources Ltd) includes articles on Northern Ireland from British journals.

For further information on the main sources of the law of Northern Ireland see: *Butterworths Legal Research Guide,* Guy Holborn, (London: Butterworths, 1993) or Dane and Thomas on *How to use a Law Library*, Cathie Cope and Philip A. Thomas. (London: Sweet & Maxwell, 3rd edition, 1995).

3.5 Republic of Ireland

Since 1922 the legislative body has been the Oireachtas or Parliament. Acts are published to a pattern similar to Westminster, appearing first as single copies and then in annual volumes in Irish and English, for the majority of issues. Since 1984 the official versions have been supplemented by *Irish Current Law Statutes Annotated* (London: Sweet & Maxwell), which is similar to its English counterpart, except that is mainly in loose-leaf format. The indexing to *Irish Current Law Statutes Annotated* is superior to the official versions, so is to be preferred for research. There are no Irish equivalents to *Current Law Citators* so it is difficult to check whether an Act has been amended subsequently or the wording interpreted by the courts. There is no electronic database containing the statutes or secondary legislation of the Republic of Ireland.

Secondary legislation, in the form of statutory instruments, is published by the Stationery Office, Dublin, and a copy of every instrument is sent to ten designated libraries. Recent instruments are in typescript form only in the language in which they were made (almost always English). Between 1985 and 1991 they are available as printed pamphlets only in English. Those published between 1948 and 1984 are available in bound volumes in both English and Irish versions. Indexes to statutory instruments are published by both the Stationery Office and Butterworths.

Turning to the reporting of cases, the two main general series of reports are the *Irish Reports* (Dublin: Incorporated Council of Law Reporting for Ireland) and the *Irish Law Reports Monthly* (Dublin: Irish Academic Press). There are also specialist reports. As in the English jurisdiction there is some reliance on unreported cases. The main tools for finding reported case law are the *Irish Digest,* which carries brief notes of cases arranged by subject, three general indexes to judgements from 1966 onwards, and *Irish Law Log,* (published 10 times a year) which summarises recent decisions. There is no general encyclopaedia of Irish law like *Halsbury's Laws of England.* LEXIS, the on-line database, has a library of reported Irish case law commencing with 1950, and also selected unreported cases from July 1985 onwards.

Indexes covering a limited number of Irish law periodicals as well as those of other jurisdictions include: *Index to Legal Periodicals* (New York: H.W.Wilson & Co., 11 issues p.a. - also available as a CD and on LEXIS) and *Current Law Year Books* (London: Sweet & Maxwell). During 1995 Sweet & Maxwell started publishing *Irish Current Law Monthly Digest* which, like *Current Law* mentioned above under English and Wales, provides synopses of the latest legislation, cases and an index to articles in over 300 journals.

The Incorporated Law Society of Ireland publishes an annual *Law Directory,* which also lists solicitors in Northern Ireland.

For further information on the main sources of the law of the Republic of Ireland see: *Sources of Law.* Thomas O'Malley. (Dublin: Round Hall Press, 1993). Appendix 4 of this book is a bibliography of Irish law books published since 1950. Other general sources of information on Irish legal materials include sections in *Butterworths Legal Research Guide,* Guy Holborn, (London: Butterworths, 1993) and Dane and Thomas on *How to use a Law Library,* Cathie Cope and Philip A. Thomas. (London: Sweet & Maxwell, 3rd edition, 1995).

3.6 Isle of Man

Manx law is sought mainly by those involved in company, trust and insurance law because of the island's status as a tax haven. The island has its own legislature: Tynwald, one of the oldest Parliaments in the world. Manx legislation is contained in *Statutes of the Isle of Man* which reprints primary legislation from 1417 to 1970. This is supplemented by *Acts of Tynwald* (1971-), which since 1977 has been a loose-leaf publication. Secondary legislation is issued in the form of Government circulars and is not widely available outside the island. Manx law is not contained on any electronic database. Enquiries about Manx legal sources are best directed to either the Attorney General's Chambers, Central Government Offices, Bucks Road, Douglas, Isle of Man (Tel: 01624 685455) or the Central Reference Library, Isle of Man Public Library, Ridgeway Street, Douglas, Isle of Man (Tel: 01624 623021) which offers a telephone and postal enquiry service.

Manx Law Reports (Oxford: Law Reports International) have been published since 1972, and are available in some libraries outside the island. The *Manx Law Bulletin,* prepared by the Attorney General's Chambers contains case notes and summaries of Acts of Tynwald and other legislation.

3.7 Channel Islands

Like the Isle of Man, the law of the Channel Islands is usually required by those seeking to use its status as a tax haven. The Channel Islands comprise the two bailiwicks of Jersey and Guernsey each with their own legislatures, courts and government. Alderney and Sark are dependencies of Guernsey but are distinct jurisdictions with their own legislatures and customs. The Channel Islands were originally part of the Duchy of Normandy and derive their system of law from the Normans. The legislation of each island is not widely available outside the islands and it is only comparatively recently that the decisions of the courts have been published. The law of the Channel Islands is not contained on any electronic database. For information about the laws of Jersey the Honorary Librarian of the Jersey Law Society, 18, Grenville Street, St. Helier, Jersey (01534 74343) may be able to help, but note that this a private organisation. For Guernsey, the States of Guernsey Library, Priaulx Road, Candie Road, St Peter Port, Guernsey (01481 721998) will take telephone and postal enquiries. The same applies for the Royal Court Library, Royal Court House, St Peter Port, Guernsey (01481 726161).

4. The literature of law in selected countries outside the British Isles

4.1 European Community

What is it and what are the sources of European Community law?
The terms European Union, European Community, European Communities, Common Market, Internal Market do not refer to the same organisation but are often used inter-changeably. Some definitions are required to clarify things:

- The European Union (EU), established among the 12 Member States of the time by the Maastricht Treaty of 1992, is merely a stage in the process of creating a closer union among the peoples of Europe. It adds new dimensions to the original Treaties which founded the European Communities. It does not replace them.
- The phrase 'European Communities' refers to the European Coal and Steel Community (ECSC), set up in 1952, the European Atomic Energy Community (Euratom) set up in 1958 and the European Economic Community (EEC), otherwise known as the Treaty of Rome after the city in which it was signed in 1957. Usually, when reference is made to the 'Community', it is the European Economic Community which is meant. However, for all practical purposes the other two Communities have been absorbed into the EEC. A further complication is that the Maastricht Treaty has changed the name of the European Economic Community to the 'European Community' (EC).
- The 'Common Market' is often confused with the European Community. It refers only to the freedoms and policies implemented within the Community. It excludes external relations.
- Internal Market is that part of the Common Market concerned with the free movement of goods, persons, services and capital. It was the object of the Single European Act (SEA) of 1986 and was completed at the end of 1992.

This section of the book is about the European Community (EC). EC legal information sources may be divided into primary (i.e. original) and secondary (i.e. commentary and description) - see figure 3.

The primary legislation comprises the founding treaties, later amending treaties, and the treaties of accession of the member states. The secondary legislation sets out in detail how the objectives established by the treaties are to be met.

The case law comprises the decisions of the European Court of Justice. The secondary sources comprise textbooks and periodicals.

To assist the flow of information about EC matters, the EC has set up several networks of organisations holding the documents of the EC and some with access to its official database: Celex. The Euro Info Centres (EICs) are sent a selection of the documents of the EC but usually do not hold documentation prior to their creation in 1987. European Documentation Centres (EDCs) are comprehensive collections of EC documentation open to the general public. They are based in academic institutions. EC Depository Libraries (DEPs) are major collections of EC materials. Usually they are based in national, state, or parliamentary libraries. They are found both in member states and elsewhere (e.g. the United States). There is also a network of European Reference Centres (ERCs) which have basic collections of EC documentation. They are usually based in academic institutions.

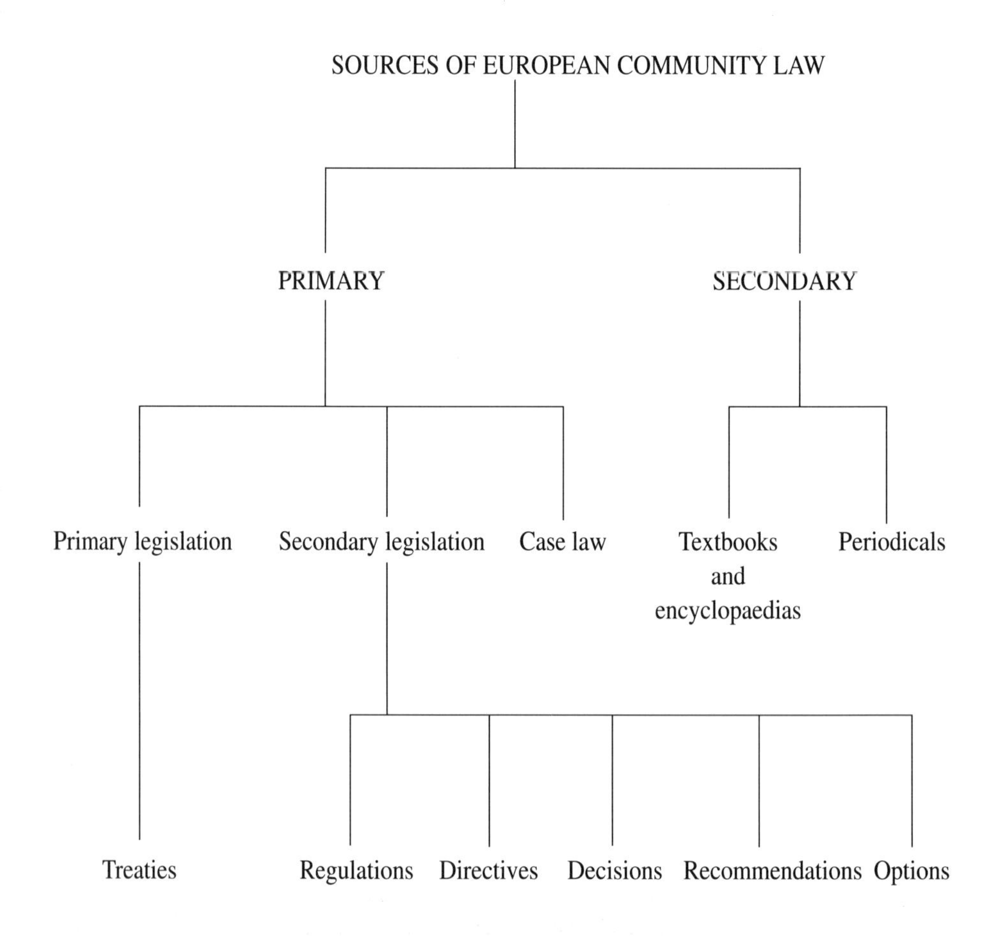

Figure 3 - The literature of European Community law

Lists of the EICs, EDCs, DEPs and ERCs are available from the Information Offices of the Commission situated in member countries. A list correct to 1989 is given in appendix 6 of the most comprehensive guide to EC literature: *The Documentation of the European Communities: a guide,* by Ian Thomson (London: Mansell, 1989). A more up to date guide to organisations holding EC Information in the UK and Ireland is given at the back of *Butterworths Legal Research Guide,* by Guy Holborn (London: Butterworths, 1993), in the Quick Reference Guide, section 9.9. EC publications can be purchased through HMSO Books (Agency Section) - see chapter 5 for contact details.

Treaties
The authorised text of the treaties and secondary legislation of the EC is not made available in separate individual publications as is the legislation of countries such as England and Wales. The official text is printed in the pages of the *Official Journal of the European* Communities (normally abbreviated to Official Journal or, simply, OJ). OJ is published almost daily and in several parts. Approved legislation is printed in the 'L' series. Community publications are usually printed in each of the languages of the member states. The covers of official EC publications are colour-coded according to the language of publication and English language publications have purple covers.

For convenience the texts of the primary legislation are brought together in a two volume work: *Treaties Establishing the European Communities, Treaties Amending these Treaties, Single European Act and Documents Concerning Accessions* (Luxembourg: Office for Official Publications of the European Communities, 1987). There is also an abridged version of this publication which omits most of the annexes. A more recent publication: *European Union: selected instruments taken from the Treaties* (Luxembourg: Office for Official Publications of the European Communities. 2 volumes. 1993) includes information on the Maastricht Treaty. Unofficial versions of the treaties are given in the following:

> *Encyclopedia of European Community Law* (London: Sweet & Maxwell) - a loose-leaf publication in 16 volumes: the text is given in volume B. The format of this publication is being changed during 1995, so check carefully
>
> *Common Market Reporter* (Bicester: CCH Editions Ltd.) - a loose-leaf publication in four volumes.
>
> *Blackstone's EC Legislation.* Edited by Nigel Foster (London: Blackstone Press, 5th ed., 1994) - a single volume reprint without annotations.

The text of the treaties is also available on a number of electronic sources: CELEX is the official legal database of the EC held on a computer in Luxembourg. The database is divided into sectors and the text of the treaties is held in Sector 2. The search language is not easy to use. EUROLAW (published by Infonorme London Information) is a CD version of the CELEX database. JUSTIS CELEX CD (published by Context Ltd) enhances the CELEX database with added text and is easier to search than the official version. It is updated quarterly, but registered users have access to JUSTIS ONLINE for more recent information. LEXIS contains the text of the treaties in its EURCOM Library - the same material as in the CELEX database.

Secondary legislation
The five different types of secondary legislation are noted in figure 3 above. Lawyers and those researching the law are usually most interested in the Regulations and Directives of the EC. The text of proposed secondary legislation appears in the *Official Journal* 'C' series. Once it has passed through the legislative process of the EC, the official text of legislation is printed in the *Official Journal* 'L' series. References to the *Official Journal* take the form:

OJ series, issue number, date of issue, page number

as in the following example:

Proposal for a Council Directive on safety glazing and glazing materials on motor vehicles and their trailers (OJ No. C95, 12.4.1990, p.1.).

The official indexes to the *Official Journal* are published monthly with an annual cumulation. They are not easy to use. A quicker way to trace the text of EC secondary legislation is to use either the *Encyclopedia of European Community Law* (London: Sweet & Maxwell) - a loose-leaf encyclopaedia presently undergoing changes to its format, or *Common Market Reporter* (Bicester: CCH Editions Ltd) - a loose-leaf encyclopaedia in four volumes, or an electronic source such as CELEX (the official EC legal database held in Luxembourg), or EUROLAW (published by Infonorme London Information), the CD version of the CELEX database, or JUSTIS CELEX CD (London: Context Ltd), or LEXIS, the EURCOM library.

A very useful commentary on the law of the EC updated each month, is contained in volumes 51 and 52 of the general encyclopaedia: *Halsbury's Laws of England* (London: Butterworths). The commentary is especially valuable because it links legislation and case law together. More details about *Halsbury's Laws* are given above.

EC Cases
The European Court of Justice (not to be confused with the European Court of Human Rights, see below) hears cases involving the interpretation of the legislation of the EC. The decisions of the court are published officially in the *Official Reports of Cases before the Court,* more popularly known as *European Court Reports* (ECR). Publication of ECR is delayed frequently by between 18 months to two years because of the importance attached to the precise and accurate translation of the judgements and opinions into all EC languages.

Unofficial reports published more rapidly are to be found in the national daily newspapers such as *The Times,* or in *Common Market Law Reports,* published by Sweet and Maxwell, or the loose-leaf encyclopaedia *Common Market Reporter* (Bicester: CCH Editions Ltd.). Electronic sources for the full text of cases are CELEX (sector 6), EUROLAW (published by Infonorme London Information) the CD version of the CELEX database or, JUSTIS CELEX CD and LEXIS, the EURCOM library. LEXIS contains not only the full text of all cases reported since the foundation of the court, but also transcripts of cases not yet reported in ECR.

Secondary sources
Both the EC and commercial publishers produce books, periodicals, booklets, pamphlets and reports on EC law. The EC itself produces SCAD, a weekly bulletin listing a wide range of EC documents and also articles from non-EC periodicals. It is available as a remote on-line database or as a Compact Disc from two providers: SCAD + CD (ELLIS Publications) or EC Infodisk (Ascot: Infonorme London Information) both containing information prepared by the EC Publications Office, updated quarterly. JUSTIS European References (London: Context Ltd) is an enhanced CD version of SCAD including material from another database: Spicers Centre for Europe.

European Access (Cambridge: Chadwyck-Healey Ltd), published bimonthly, is not confined to law but comprehensively lists new EC publications, comment in newspapers, journals and books about the EC, including legislative developments.

European Legal Journals Index (Hebden Bridge: Legal Information Resources Ltd) lists articles contained in over 200 law periodicals published in the United Kingdom. It commenced in January 1993 in both paper and electronic formats. Prior to 1993 EC law articles were indexed in a sister publication: *Legal Journals Index.*

Both *Current Law Monthly Digest* and *European Current Law* (both London: Sweet & Maxwell) index EC periodical articles.

To trace the names of leading law firms in Europe use *Law Firms in Europe* edited by John Pritchard (London: Legalease, Annual). It focuses on firms which undertake commercial legal work.

4.2 European Court of Human Rights

This court should not be confused with the European Court of Justice (see above). In 1950 the Council of Europe (an international organisation comprising all the non-Communist states of Europe) drafted the European Convention for the Protection of Human Rights and Fundamental Freedoms.

The Convention set up a Commission of Human Rights to investigate complaints, and the European Court of Human Rights to decide on cases brought to it. The court, which sits in Strasbourg, publishes official reports. Unofficial reports of a selection of cases are published by the European Law Centre at Sweet & Maxwell, in a series entitled *European Human Rights Reports* (EHRR). It is probable that only the larger UK university law libraries will subscribe to one or both of these publications. LEXIS contains in its EURCOM library the full text of all EHRR reports since 1960 and unreported cases from October 1980 onwards.

If any European Human Rights Court case is reported in United Kingdom law reports then the case will be indexed and summarised in *Current Law Monthly Digest*. If the report has appeared in one of the daily newspapers, then it will be indexed in *Daily Law Reports Index*. For more details of both these publications see above.

For further information on the main sources of international human rights law see: *Butterworths Legal Research Guide*, Guy Holborn, (London: Butterworths, 1993) or Dane and Thomas on *How to use a Law Library,* Cathie Cope and Philip A. Thomas. (London: Sweet & Maxwell, 3rd edition, 1995) or *Sources of Law,* Thomas O'Malley, (Dublin: Round Hall Press, 1993).

4.3 Other European countries

Vive la différence!

It is not only the language barrier which lawyers and LIS staff working on legal problems need to surmount when looking for the law of countries on continental Europe. The legal systems of these countries are based on different principles from those of England and Wales, Northern Ireland and the Irish Republic. They are based on either the Civil law system or the Socialist system. Some basic differences between the systems were noted above.

Partly as a result of European integration and the end of the Cold War, and partly as a result of improvements in transport and telecommunications, people, goods and services now flow more easily between European countries. These transactions and any resulting litigation (the resolution of disputes through the courts) will require LIS staff to have a basic knowledge of the sources of the 'domestic' law of European countries (i.e. the law created within a country rather than the law created by an international organisation such as the European Community).

Legislation

In Civil law systems a distinctive feature is that much of the legislation of a country is codified. The structure of the Napoleonic codification of the early nineteenth century has been followed by many countries, consisting of five codes: the Civil Code, the Code of Civil Procedure, the Commercial Code, the Penal Code and the Code of Criminal Procedure. In addition to these there are often consolidating codes which bring together numerous statutes and decrees relevant to a particular specialised subject: for example, labour law, fiscal law. To date, France has 58 codes. Commercially published versions of the codes are the most easily available. An annotated version of the French codes: *Petits Codes Dalloz* (Dalloz), is updated annually. There are numerous editions of the German codes, some which contain only the bare text of the code itself, for example: Beck's *Rote Textausgabe* (Berlin: C H Beck) - known as 'red text editions' - or others which are highly authoritative commentaries, such as Staudinger's *Kommentar zum Bürgerlichen Gesetzbuch mit Einführungsgesetz und Nebengesetzen* (Berlin: Schweizer) for the German civil code.

Translations of many codes have been made, especially of the commercial codes. The Council of Europe has produced a useful guide to translations of European laws: *Bibliography of translations of codes and other laws of private law* (Strasbourg: Council of Europe, 2nd ed., 1975). *Commercial Laws of Europe* (London: Sweet & Maxwell) is a monthly periodical which provides the full text in both the original language and in English translation, of major topical legislation from across Europe. As its title suggests, it covers subjects such as banking and insurance, product liability, companies, stock exchange and consumer protection. *Digest of Commercial Laws of the World* (New York: Oceana) is an 11 volume loose-leaf work, providing summaries of the law for over 100 countries.

A number of European countries have set up computerised legal research systems. LEXIS, which is available to British users, has the full-text of all the French codes (58) and a large number of other associated materials (the whole in French, of course) in its LOIREG library. The German full-text system: JURIS is starting to be marketed in Britain.

Keeping up to date with changes in the laws of European countries (both West and East) has been made easier since the beginning of 1992 with the publication of *European Current Law* (London: Sweet & Maxwell). It is similar to its older sister: *Current Law Monthly Digest,* in that it summarises changes to legislation but does not provide the full text.

Case law

The position of case law in the legal systems of continental European countries varies from that in the United Kingdom. The reasons need not concern us here. However, a continental lawyer still has a need to refer to the published decisions of the courts, even though the decisions may not be used in quite the same way as they would be by a Common law practitioner.

Official and unofficial series of reports co-exist. Probably of more interest to English readers are the full-text translations of key cases provided by *European*

Commercial Cases (London: Sweet & Maxwell), a bi-monthly periodical. It provides English translations of the major commercial and business law decisions of the national European courts. There is no publication in any other area of law like it. Keeping up to date with new decisions in all areas of law is accomplished with *European Current Law* (London: Sweet & Maxwell) which, since January 1992, has summarised selected judgements from the courts of 30 countries from both Western and Eastern Europe.

The only court decisions from European countries which are widely available outside the country of origin in electronic form, are the decisions of the French courts. LEXIS has libraries of French private and public cases (in French) commencing at various dates, mainly from the 1960's onwards.

Secondary sources
For periodical articles on the law of civil law jurisdictions, the best source is *Index to Foreign Legal Periodicals* (Berkeley: University of California Press). It is also available as a CD from SilverPlatter. Most of the articles noted will not be in English. For commentary on foreign law, loose-leaf encyclopaedias such as *Company Law in Europe* (London: Butterworths), which provides a commentary on the law of a number of European countries, with footnotes to original legal sources, will be very useful.

To trace the names of law firms in Europe use the directory edited by John Pritchard mentioned at the end of the section on the European Community above.

4.4 Australia

The Constitution of the Commonwealth of Australia came into effect in 1901 and created a Federal Government and six States. Since then two further States have achieved self-government, so bringing the number of separate jurisdictions with their own bodies of law to nine. Primary Federal legislation is published as Acts of the Parliament of the Commonwealth of Australia, by the Australian Government Publishing Service, Canberra, firstly as individual copies and later in annual, bound volumes with the Acts arranged in the order of receiving assent. If an Act is subsequently amended a reprint pamphlet is issued but without the authority of Parliament. Early legislation has been consolidated in a set of 12 bound volumes entitled: *Acts of the Australian Parliament 1901-1973,* which provide a complete statement of the law up to that date, the Acts arranged in alphabetical order by title. Similar arrangements apply for secondary legislation, which is first printed as individual pamphlets, then, if amendments are passed, reprint pamphlets are issued. Finally, there is a consolidation of 1956.

Individual States have their own primary and secondary legislation, each with their own publishing idiosyncrasies. Keeping up to date with Federal and State legislative developments can be achieved by using one of two rival publications: *Australian Legal Monthly Digest* (Sydney, The Law Book Co.,) or *Australian Current Law* (Sydney, Butterworths). Few university law libraries in Britain stock Australian legislation or the current awareness services. To date, no Australian legislation is available in electronic format.

The Australian court system can be confusing both in its structure and the names given to different courts, especially for people more familiar with the English system. The High Court is the supreme Federal court and is also the highest court of appeal for the State supreme courts. The authorised reports of the High Court are the *Commonwealth Law Reports* which are widely available in British university law libraries. The *Australian Law Journal Reports* carry advance reports of High Court cases. Another widely available series of law reports is *Australian Law Reports* which covers reports of cases heard in the Federal courts and major cases from the State supreme courts. Each State has its own authorised series of law reports in addition. A very limited selection of Australian case law is available on LEXIS in the Commonwealth cases library.

Halsbury's Laws of Australia (Sydney, Butterworths) is similar to *Halsbury's Laws of England* in aiming to provide a narrative statement of the law arranged according to subject. The 28 volume set is due to be completed in 1995/6, and will cover both Federal and State laws. *Australian Current Law* acts as the updating service for *Halsbury's Laws of Australia.* Australian lawyers use a similar system of citation to legal materials as employed in England and Wales (see page 20, above).

To find the names of lawyers and law firms in Australia use the *Australian Legal Directory* (annual, published by the Australian Document Exchange Pty. Ltd. and distributed by Butterworths).

For further information on the main sources of Australian law and how to use them see: *Legal Research: Materials and Methods.* Enid Campbell (Sydney: The Law Book Co., 3rd ed., 1988) or *Concise Legal Research.* Robert Watt (Sydney,: Federation Press, 1993).

4.5 Canada

Canada, like Australia, has a constitution and federal and provincial legal materials. But, to complicate matters further the legal system of one of the nine provinces: Quebec, is mixed, containing elements drawn from the civil system of France as well as the common law system. Since the Constitution Act 1867 Quebec has always published its statutes in English and French but other provinces have done so only from more recent date.

Canada Gazette (Ottawa, Queen's Printer, 1974-), is a daily bulletin containing the text of Federal legislation (both primary and secondary) as it is passed. Provincial gazettes fulfil the same purpose. Statutes are republished as annual volumes. *Revised Statutes of Canada,* 1985 (Ottawa, Queen's Printer, 1988-) is a loose-leaf consolidation of federal primary legislation. The most recent consolidation of secondary legislation is *Consolidated Regulations of Canada,* 1978. Carswell, a private publisher, produces a *Consolidated Index to the Regulations of Canada,* with monthly supplements. Few university law libraries in the Britain will hold these materials. The Canadian based QUICKLAW or QL database contains the full text of some federal and provincial legislation but it is not known whether any UK law library has access to it.

As to the reports of cases heard in the courts, the *Dominion Law Reports* are the only publication reporting both federal and provincial cases. The title is widely available in British law libraries. In addition, and less widely available, are official series of law reports for each province and an increasing number of specialist series covering particular subjects. Canadian lawyers use a similar system of citation to legal materials as lawyers in England and Wales (see p 20, above). LEXIS coverage of Canadian case law is very limited. Three purely Canadian databases: QUICKLAW, Infomart Online and Canadian Law Online also contain either the full text or digests of Federal and provincial decisions, but it is not known whether any law library in Britain has access to them.

To find the names of lawyers and firms working in Canada use the *Martindale Hubbell Canadian and International Lawyers*. The *Canadian Law List* (annual, Canadian Law Book Inc.) gives a comprehensive listing of all Canadian courts, judges and lawyers.

For further information on the main sources of Canadian law and how to use them see: *Banks on Using a Law Library.* Margaret A Banks and Karen E H Foti. (Toronto: Carswell, 6th ed., 1994).

4.6 United States

Although the United States is part of the same legal family as the United Kingdom (the common law family) there are important differences. It is essential to be aware of the large number of jurisdictions in the United States - there is a federal system consisting of a legislature, a hierarchy of courts and an administration all with law making functions. In addition each of the 50 states (plus the District of Columbia) has a legislature, hierarchy of courts and administrative agencies producing 'law'. So, before you start a search for a particular piece of legislation or case ensure you know whether it is federal or state law that you require. If searching by subject, rather than for a specific document, things become more complicated still, because both federal and state law may be involved.

The United States Constitution is printed in several different publications: the Library of Congress publishes a version, but probably the most widely available in law libraries is the version found in the *United States Code.* The *United States Code* is a subject arrangement of the general laws (the Constitution and the Acts of Congress) of the United States. It is published in three different versions: those by the private publishers: West Publishing Co., and the Lawyers' Cooperative, are the most valuable because they include extensive annotations or notes. The *United States Code* is available on CD-ROM from a number of different producers. State legislation follows a pattern similar to the federal: individual pieces of legislation are later consolidated into codes. Although individual states are relatively autonomous a measure of uniformity is desirable. To this end several official organisations have produced uniform laws or model codes. The *Uniform Commercial Code* was the first produced and probably the most widely consulted. It has been adopted with only minor local variation by every state except Louisiana. All uniform laws are collected in the *Uniform Laws Annotated* (St. Paul, West Publishing Co., 1976-).

Turning to the reports of cases heard in the courts, the decisions of the Supreme Court are published officially under the title *United States Supreme Court Reports.* Two privately published series: the *Lawyers' Edition* (published by the Lawyers' Co-operative) and the *Supreme Court Reporter* (published by West Publishing Co.,), cover the same material, the former including very full annotations to each case. A practical difficulty which requires a little patience to master is that the page numbering of the two unofficial versions in no way corresponds to the official version, though the volume numbers of the official series are printed in small type face on the spines of the *Lawyers' Edition* and the *Supreme Court Reporter.*

Below the Supreme Court are the District Courts of the federal jurisdiction, of which there is at least one in each state. Appeals from the District Courts go to the Court of Appeals and from there to the Supreme Court. Reports of cases heard in all these federal courts and some other specialist ones besides, are published in the federal parts of the *National Reporter System* (West Publishing Co.,). This *System* also includes 'regional reporters' containing the reports of decisions of State courts. This vast publishing venture provides a standardised format and the most comprehensive coverage in paper format of the decisions of the United States Courts both federal and state. In the United Kingdom, electronic access to this huge publishing output is most easily available through the LEXIS computer database in Dayton, Ohio. Electronic access to the West Publishing Co., database: WESTLAW is also possible but not as widely available outside the United States.

To find the names of lawyers and firms working in the United States use the *Martindale-Hubbell Law Directory* (12 volumes). The directory is loaded on LEXIS and is also available as a CD (in Europe from Bowker-Saur Ltd (UK)), so enabling sophisticated searching not possible with the printed version.

In the United Kingdom only the larger university law libraries will have collections including some United States publications. Unfortunately the providers of the LEXIS database require university law libraries to restrict use of the database only to members of the university.

There are many guides to researching United States law, but they are primarily written for law students or practising lawyers rather than non-lawyers. The following British publication attempts to provide general hints on technique rather than a detailed explanation of the most extensive legal publishing machine in the world and may prove a useful, first step source of advice: *United States Legal Research.* Robert Logan. (Hebden Bridge: Legal Information Resources Ltd, 1990).

4.7 International Law

What is it and what are the main sources?
International law is the system of rules and principles that govern the international relations between states. Primarily, the rules are created by states, for states. They cover almost every aspect of inter-state activity: international telecommunications, postal services, the carriage of goods and passengers by air and the transfer of money. In addition, there are rules covering nationality, extradition, the use of armed force and the rights of the individual. The enforcement of these rules is carried out by the International Court of Justice, which sits in The Hague, Netherlands. It produces official reports of its 'awards' - the word it uses for its decisions. States create international law through international conventions or treaties. Treaties can be bilateral (between two states) or multilateral (between many). Treaties range from those defining the status of a territory, such as the Joint Declaration of the British and Chinese Governments on the future of Hong Kong which came into force in 1985, to the multilateral treaties such as the Antarctic Treaty of 1959 regulating the use of the landspace.

Terminology can be puzzling, for the words Convention, Covenant, Charter, Act, Statute and Protocol are all used to refer to treaties.

In December 1946 the United Nations started publishing the full text of every treaty entered into by any of its members. The United Nations Treaty Series (UNTS) now runs to over 1,000 volumes. Treaties are published not in the order of signature or ratification, but in order of registration with the United Nations. It is the most comprehensive collection of treaties but, unfortunately, it is nearly seven years behind in publishing the texts of treaties. The best source for the text of recent treaties is *International Legal Materials,* a journal which reproduces the texts of many relatively obscure treaties and other agreements before they are officially available elsewhere.

To trace a law firm, chambers or law society in another part of the world use *Kimes International Law Directory* (London: Longman, Annual), which gives contact details of over 900 organisations. This directory also provides a brief synopsis of the legal system in operation in each country listed and the languages used in court and legal documents. Two other directories which perform similar functions but omit the synopsis, are *Butterworths International Law Directory* (London: Butterworths) and the *International Law List* (Corpor-Mordaunt).

Where will you find these publications?
Universities where international law forms part of the undergraduate law course are likely to have *International Legal Materials.* Only a few law libraries will take the UN Treaty Series. The UN has set up a network of over 300 Depository Libraries world-wide. These depositories (which are often national or university or other large research libraries), receive either a full or partial set of UN publications determined by the UN, in the official language of their choice. Depository libraries are expected to provide free public access to the collections. The UN issues a *'List of Depository Libraries receiving United Nations Material'* from time to time. Treaties to which the United Kingdom is a signatory are reproduced in the Treaty Series which is a part of the series of Command Papers, published by HMSO. These may be traced through the HMSO catalogue, available in most large UK university and public libraries. Many UK university libraries will have sets of the UK Treaty Series. UN publications can be purchased through HMSO Books (Agency Section) - see chapter 5 for contact details.

There are a number of indexes to treaties, of which the following two are the most useful. *Multilateral Treaties: Index and Current Status* by Bowman and Harris - the main volume published by Butterworths in 1984, with cumulative supplements published by the University of Nottingham Treaty Centre (latest supplement published 1992) - covers nearly 1,000 of the most significant treaties from 1856 onwards. *Index of British Treaties* (London: HMSO) is a four volume work covering all treaties entered into by the United Kingdom between 1101 and 1988. Using these indexes it is possible to identify in which sources the text of a particular treaty is published, and the nations which are signatories.

In 1995 the vast documentary output of the United Nations will be searchable using UNBIS Plus on CD-ROM. The CD will include bibliographic files for some 450,000 records, a full text file of the resolutions of the General Assembly and fact and reference files on a large number of other matters. Unfortunately the CD will not contain the full text of treaties. LEXIS contains an international law library with a file of the full text of the periodical *International Legal Materials* from January 1980 onwards and other files of treaties relating to the United States. For specialists, LEXIS has a file entitled *Basic Documents of International Economic Law,* containing documents on international trade.

For further information on the main sources of international law see: *Butterworths Legal Research Guide,* Guy Holborn, (London: Butterworths, 1993) or Dane and Thomas on *How to use a Law Library,* Cathie Cope and Philip A. Thomas. (London: Sweet & Maxwell, 3rd edition, 1995) or *Sources of Law,* Thomas O'Malley, (Dublin: Round Hall Press, 1993).

4.8 Conclusion

Finding the law is not easy! Even practising lawyers and law students have difficulty on occasions, which is why many law firms and universities have specialist law librarians to assist. If you are not able to find the information you require from this brief and basic guide, look back at section 2.1 and use one of the law library directories mentioned to trace the closest source of help to you. Better still, if you are in regular need of legal information join your national special interest association or group for law librarians (see the contact list at the end of chapter 5). Happy hunting!

5. Contacts

N.B. To dial telephone numbers in the UK from overseas dial the international prefix, then 44, then the area code in the UK without the initial 0, then the number.

5.1 Databases

EC Infodisk and EUROLAW
Infonorme London Information (ILI)
Index House
Ascot
Berks SL5 7EU
Tel: 01344 874343
Fax: 01344 291194

HyperTax and HyperVAT
HMSO Electronic Publishing
Room 2F, St. Crispins
Duke Street
Norwich NR3 1PD
Tel: 01603 695726
Fax: 01603 696501

Justis
Context Ltd
Tranley House
Fleet Road
London NW3 2QW
Tel: 0171 267 7055
Fax: 0171 267 2745

Lawtel
Lawrence Impey
Lawtel Product Manager
c/o Centaur Communications Ltd
St Giles House, 50 Poland Street
London W1V 4AX
Tel: 0171 287 9800
Fax: 0171 734 1886

Legal Journals Index, European Legal Journals Index, Daily Law Reports Index
Legal Information Resources Ltd
Elphin House, 1 New Road
Mytholmroyd, Hebden Bridge
West Yorkshire HX7 5DZ
Tel: 01422 886277
Fax: 01422 886250

LIR has recently been acquired by Sweet & Maxwell. All the databases noted above and others not featured in this book are available in hard copy and electronic format, either as CD-ROM, or as a fortnightly updated tape to run on in-house computer information systems. LIR also publish an Australian Legal Journals Index and a Canadian Legal Journals Index.

LEXIS
Butterworths
Halsbury House
35 Chancery Lane
London WC2A 1EL
Tel: 0171 400 2500
Fax: 0171 400 2941

In addition to the wide range of LEXIS full text libraries featured in this book, LEXIS contains libraries of Australian, Canadian, New Zealand, and United States law. Butterworths offer a research bureau service for organisations which do not subscribe to LEXIS but who occasionally require searches undertaken.

LEXIS is available in Northern Ireland through ITELIS Ltd., Fanum House, Great Victoria Street, Belfast (Tel: 01232 247 007) and in the Republic of Ireland through the same firm at 29, Fleet Street, Dublin 2 (Tel: +(353) 1 671 735).

Link (Legal Information Network)
28-30 Cato Street
London W1H 5HS
Tel: 0171 396 9292
Fax: 0171 396 9300

SilverPlatter Information Ltd.
(not the name of a database but the firm which provides several law-related CD-ROMs).
10 Barley Mow Passage
Chiswick, London W4 4PH
Tel: 0181 995 8242
Fax: 0181 995 5159

UKOP
Chadwyck-Healey Ltd
The Quorum
Barnwell Road
Cambridge CB5 8SW
Tel: 01223 215514 (Sales)
01223 215515 (Customer Service)
Fax: 01223 215513

5.2 Major law publishers noted in this book

Blackstone Press Ltd
9-15 Aldine Street
London W12 8AW
Tel: 0181 740 1173
Fax: 0181 743 2292

Butterworths & Co (Publishers) Ltd
Sales and Customer Service Departments
Halsbury House
35 Chancery Lane
London WC2A 1EL
Tel: 0171 400 2968 (UK customers)
0171 400 2971 (Overseas customers)
Fax 0171 400 2969 (UK customers)
0171 400 2972 (Overseas customers)
Direct order line (24 hours) 0171 400 2973

Butterworths Bookshop
Halsbury House
35 Chancery Lane
London WC2A 1EL
Tel: 0171 400 2867/8
Fax: 0171 400 2870

Butterworths Scottish Showroom
4 Hill Street
Edinburgh EH2 3JZ
Tel: 0131 225 7828
Fax: 0131 220 1833

Butterworth (Ireland) Ltd
26 Upper Ormond Quay
Dublin 7
Eire
Tel: +(353) 1 873 1555
Fax: +(353) 1 873 1876

CCH Editions Ltd
Telford Road
Bicester
Oxon. OX6 0XD
Tel: 01869 253300
Fax: 01869 245814

W Green & Son Ltd
2-10 St Giles Street
Edinburgh EH1 1PU
Tel: 0131 225 4879
Fax: 0131 225 2104

Her Majesty's Stationery Office
Publications Centre (mail, fax and phone orders only)
PO Box 276
London SW8 5DT
Tel: 0171 873 9090 (orders only)
Tel: 0171 873 0011 (enquiries)
Fax: 0171 873 8200

HMSO (Agency Section) (for EC and UN publications)
HMSO Publications Centre
51 Nine Elms Lane
London SW1B 5DR
Tel: 0171 873 9090
Fax: 0171 873 8463

HMSO Bookshop
49 High Holborn
London WC1V 6HB
Tel: 0171-873 0011 (counter service only)
Fax: 0171 831 1326 (counter service only)

HMSO Bookshop
16 Arthur Street
Belfast BT1 4GD
Tel: 01232 238451
Fax: 01232 235401

Overseas orders from countries where there is no HMSO stockist or distributor, may be placed in writing to:

HMSO Books
PO Box 276
London SW8 5DT

Legalease
28-33 Cato Street
London W1H 5HS
Tel: 0171 396 9292

Lord Chancellor's Department Library Services
Supreme Court Library
Queen's Building
Royal Courts of Justice
Strand
London WC2 2LL
Tel: 0171 936 6587

The Round Hall Press
Kill Lane
Blackrock
County Dublin
Ireland
Tel: +(353) 1 2892922
Fax: +(353) 1 2893072

Stationery Office, Dublin
Government Publications Sales Office
Sun Alliance House
Molesworth
Dublin 2
Eire

Sweet & Maxwell
Cheriton House
North Way
Andover
Hampshire SP1 5BE

Tel: 01264 342730 (Customers from London and Home Counties)
01264 342740 (... Central and Southern England and Wales)
01264 342750 (... Northern England and Ireland)
01264 342828 (International book orders and information)
01264 334714 (International subscription orders and information)
Fax: 01264 342723 (Customers from London and Home Counties)
01264 342723 (... Central and Southern England and Wales)
01264 342723 (... Northern England and Ireland)
01264 342761 (International book orders and information)
01264 342723 (International subscription orders and information)

5.3 Bookshops

Hammicks Bookshops Ltd
Mail Order and Subscription Department
Hounslow House
730 London Road
Hounslow
Middlesex TW3 1PD
Tel: 0181 899 5070 (24 hours)
Fax: 0181 899 5075 (24 hours)

Orders can be placed at any of Hammicks Bookshops but a wider range of law stock is held at the two Legal Bookshops:

Hammicks Legal Bookshop
191-192 Fleet Street
London EC4A 2AH
Tel: 0171 405 5711
Fax: 0171 831 9849

Hammicks Legal Bookshop
Trinity Court
16 John Dalton Street
Manchester M2 6HY
Tel: 0161 832 5557
Fax: 0161 832 2189

Law Notes Lending Library
25-26 Chancery Lane
London WC2A 1NB
Tel: 0171 405 0780/6151

5.4 Special Interest Associations and Groups

British and Irish Association of Law Librarians (BIALL)
Susan Frost
Administrator
11 Lamintone Drive
Leamington Spa
Warwickshire CV32 6SJ
Tel: 01926 430000

The Association was founded in 1969 to promote the better administration and exploitation of law libraries and legal information units. Associate membership is available to individuals and institutions not engaged in the provision or exploitation of legal literature but who support the aims of the Association. The Association publishes a quarterly journal: *The Law Librarian,* a quarterly *Newsletter* for members on Association business and new developments in the legal information world and other publications which assist libraries and users exploit legal information. The Association runs a 'Gift and Exchange' scheme through which librarians advertise publications for disposal (often for only the cost of postage) or sale. This is a very useful way of acquiring back numbers cheaply. The annual conference is well supported, not only by the membership but by commercial exhibitors. Local and regional groups of BIALL meet in various parts of the UK including London, Birmingham, Bristol and Sheffield. The organisation and meetings of these groups are very informal.

City Law Librarians Group (UK)
Ms S. Ashton
The Library
Theodore Goddard Solicitors
150 Aldersgate Street
London EC1A 4EJ
Tel: 0171 606 8855

American Association of Law Libraries (AALL)
53 W Jackson Blvd. Suite 940
Chicago
IL 60604
Tel: +(1) 312 939 4764
Fax: +(1) 312 431 1097

Australian Law Librarians Association
PO Box E40
Queen Victoria Terrace
Canberra
ACT 2600
Australia